LEADING IN THE NEXT NORMAL

*A Guide to Building an Engaged,
Resilient and Agile Virtual Workforce*

R. Michael Anderson, MBA, MA

Executive Joy! Publishing
SAN DIEGO, CALIFORNIA

Leading in the Next Normal: A Guide to Building an Engaged, Resilient and Agile Virtual Workforce

R. Michael Anderson
Executive Joy! Publishing
2 Holmwood Heights
Kings Road
Haslemere, Surrey
GU27 2QD
United Kingdom

www.RMichaelAnderson.com
www.LeadingintheNextNormal.com
info@executivejoy.com

Ordering Information:
Quantity sales. Special discounts are available on quantity purchases by corporations, associations, and others. For details, contact us at info@executivejoy.com.

Leading in the Next Normal / R. Michael Anderson. —1st ed.
ISBN: 978-0-9906605-3-8

*Dedicated to the ones
who have taught me my next level of
leadership, followship, and love: Anna, Isaac,
Marvel, Bear, Hiro & Gaia*

Contents

Preface

This is a call to leaders. You are needed now more than ever.

The new year ordinarily brings excitement, anticipation and new resolutions for the year ahead... swiftly followed by a bitter hangover and regret for overindulging.

December 31st, 2019, was no different. The promise of not only a new year but a new decade was in the air. Who could have predicted how bad the 2020 hangover would be?

This year we have experienced a life-altering global pandemic, and all that entails. The sobering daily death toll, collective anxiety, enforced lockdowns, social distancing, unemployment, working from home for months at a time, furlough schemes, national toilet roll shortages and fundamental changes in everyday life have become our daily norm.

As if that wasn't enough, we've had a dose of divisive elections, overarching political instability, Brexit and natural disasters too. It makes 2020 a year to remember - or forget - and, whether we like it or not, a defining moment for leaders.

This is not what you signed up for when you accepted your leadership role. However, you're now in a position to affect real change.

With leadership comes a responsibility that is larger than ourselves.

People look to you to see how you respond to these trials. You are a role model. Your team, your company and even your friends and family, are invested in how you handle the situation.

It's time to rise to this challenge, YOU are part of the solution.

It's time to dig deep, bring your absolute best and LEAD. Positive, strong leaders are imperative to create and ensure stability, both in business and in society. I'm not suggesting it will be easy, but it is doable.

With the right guidance, the tenacity to implement the tool kit, and the confidence to know that you can, you will make it through this.

My goal is to provide you with the mindset, tools, and support to carve your way through this extraordinary time.

Introduction

I was living in Copenhagen when the planes collided into the World Trade Centre on September 11th, 2001.

At the time, I was thousands of miles away from my hometown in California, working in Denmark for a North American based software company as their European representative.

I was glued to the TV, watching the events unfold on CNN with horror and a sick feeling in my stomach. I turned to my Danish girlfriend and said that we would remember this day for the rest of our lives.

That next week was surreal and immeasurably hard. However, like all tragedies, it was met with incredible humanity.

A day or two after 9/11, I was on the phone to one of my colleagues. He was stuck at our Vancouver HQ with a large proportion of the sales team. They were there for a multi-day sales meeting, but all air travel was frozen for a few days following the attacks. They were stranded in Vancouver.

I asked him what was going on up there, he said: "we're all pretty shocked, though Ken has been on the phone non-stop."

Ken was a senior sales guy at the company. I had always looked up to him, both as a business person and as a human being.

I replied, "Really? Why? Who's he been talking to?" I was surprised as no one was going to be worried about the multi-million dollar accounting software packages that we sold at a time like this.

He told me, "he's just reaching out to all his customers and prospects and checking in. He isn't talking about any business. He's asking if they are OK, if anyone they know got caught in the attacks, and just letting them know that he's thinking about them."

I have to be honest, the young Michael didn't totally get this, "and what are they saying?" I asked.

"They are so appreciative. Ken's been talking to some of them for an hour or so. Not business, just person to person."

That's the type of person Ken was, the kind that really cared. He wasn't calling his clients to sell a product. He truly cared about them as people, and they could feel that from his behaviour and how he reached out over those few days.

This experience still affects how I respond to unimaginable adversities today.

I've reflected on that moment many times throughout my life. As I've gotten older, wiser, and as I experience more seemingly impossible periods, I understand a little more each time.

What people need from their leaders is humanity.

The investment of your time, energy, and care will pay you back in performance, loyalty, and trust more than any other investment you can make in your business.

This book is going to walk you through what you need to do to get that payback.

Not only is it good for your bottom line, but it is the right and human thing to do; a real win-win.

How do I know that?

I took what I learned from Ken, plus a few other significant "lessons disguised as punches in the face" moments.

In 2003, I moved to Singapore for a new job. My entire sales team wound up quitting because of my arrogant behaviour - that was a sharp learning curve.

Another time that sticks out in my mind was when I started my first business. I had to deal with a nasty lawsuit that I struggled with personally, so much so that it sent me into a depression.

With each experience, I learned valuable lessons about what I needed to do to survive when stuff hits the proverbial fan.

As a result, when the great recession came around in 2007, I was ready. I knew the moves to make, and my businesses (at the time I owned and ran two) both doubled in revenue and profit, at a time when many others in my industry shrunk or went out of business.

I have been working, managing, and leading remotely for over 20 years.

My experiences drove me to write this book. It will help you as the leader, your team as people, and your company to get through this challenging time - healthy, happy, and profitably.

About Me

I've shared a part of my journey already, but here's a little more to round it out.

After starting my career as a programmer, I climbed the corporate ladder and became both a CFO and an international VP. I then started four businesses myself, sold two and acquired another.

I know that all can sound fun and glamorous, but I struggled with leadership at first. I was a decent manager, and I understood business and technology, but I did not know anything about emotional intelligence, communicating, and leading.

This caused real issues for me professionally and personally. As we grew, my lack of leadership was exposed. People quit, we lost customers, and I got into legal trouble.

I suffered from a big dose of imposter syndrome as I constantly doubted myself, and my negative self-talk was off the charts.

I hired business coaches; I took leadership training; I read management books until my eyes bled.

I went on to earn a Master's Degree in Psychology - I really wanted to get to the fundamentals of what made myself and others tick.

I can honestly say that my Psychology degree (and later, my neuroscience training) impacted my leadership abilities more than anything else I've done.

Once I started applying what I had learned, my companies really took off. We made the Inc. 5000 list a few years in a row, we were voted the #1 best place to work, and I was named Social Entrepreneur of the Year.

That was on the outside - my inner world transformed too. In the past, being a leader had smothered me with crippling pressure, and it just felt like I was babysitting the people who worked for me. However, after applying all my training and new-found knowledge, it became fun, graceful and fulfilling.

I was able to create a fantastic culture.

I focused on empowering my team, they then performed at an extremely high level while I handled the strategy. We were delivering value to our customers, and we were able to give back to the community.

I was starting to receive media exposure from the success of my companies. Other leaders were taking notice; I was approached time and time again to help them achieve the same transformation and results with their own businesses.

I really enjoyed that, it was so rewarding to be able to make a difference that way. So I sold my software companies and changed my career track.

I believe that leadership is a force for good.

When I was president of one of the California chapters of Conscious Capitalism in 2015, I got to see how a business run the "right" way can genuinely make a positive impact.

Now I teach leaders all around the world how to evolve as people and become more decisive leaders.

The unique experience I have led to Stanford University inviting me to work with their startup ecosystem and PwC asked me to work with them and their high potential clients. I have also worked with Microsoft, Salesforce and Uber to level up their leaders.

It is this drive, this tenacity, and this passion for positive leadership in business that has led me to write this book.

Using This Book

This book is written for the leaders, teams, and organizations that are going through the most extreme changes. I'm talking about the ones that have been traditionally office-based and are now having to adapt to working in a fully remote or hybrid (combination of remote and in-office) workforce.

The book consists of four main sections plus an appendix.

Part 1 is about you, the leader. You need to be at your best, and this chapter will give you the tools to manage yourself and level up your mindset. You will learn how to increase resilience and find the clarity you need to thrive during this otherwise challenging time.

Part 2 is dedicated to your team's mental and emotional health. You can't do much if your team is struggling. This section will give you direction on how to accurately gauge where they are at and how to support your team with what they need to be strong, healthy, and engaged.

Part 3 is about team performance. Remote teams can perform at as high a level - or even higher - than they were in office. Learn the tools, strategies and tactics to get the most from your team.

Part 4 talks about the "go-forward" strategy companies need to be putting in place to support their growth, goals, and people.

Finally, the appendix is dedicated to "The Healthy Leader". This section is a lifestyle guide to make sure you are doing what you need to support your own physical, mental, and emotional health.

The 12 Principles

Throughout this book I will be highlighting my fundamental principles to help your business survive this pandemic.

- » Principle 1: You can't sprint a marathon.
- » Principle 2: You don't find out about mental health issues until it's too late.
- » Principle 3: Care about the person and they'll care about their job.
- » Principle 4: Leadership is personal now.
- » Principle 5: Earn the right to have the real conversations.
- » Principle 6: Highlight, promote and even manufacture positivity.
- » Principle 7: Run tight meetings. Period.
- » Principle 8: Empowered accountability leads to a strong culture.
- » Principle 9: Focus on results and outcomes, not on time or process.
- » Principle 10: Your culture, agility, and people are your long-term competitive advantages.
- » Principle 11: Unwavering pragmatic optimism fuels the rest of the strategy.
- » Principle 12: Everyone wants to be a great team member, it's your job to let them.

The Survey

I sent out a survey in the latter half of 2020, consisting of both multiple-choice and open-ended questions. I followed this up with one-on-one interviews with both leaders and teams.

This book is a multi-faceted approach to developing the tools and skills required to succeed. The guidance you get here isn't just from my experience, it's based on real-time evidence and contains true best-practises from people who are in the trenches, just like you.

These first-hand experiences document how real people are coping with the same real situations you may find yourself in. These studies show what people have tried, what is (and isn't) working and why.

The Community

My personal purpose is to make a positive difference in the world for leaders. It's through a community that leaders can get that "missing something" that creates lasting value.

That's why I have a group that everyone with a copy of the book is invited to join.

Go to tiny.cc/leadersgroup and follow the instructions to join other driven, successful leaders who are committed to being the best leader they can.

You will find more content, inspiration, and some cool, like-minded people to network with alongside myself.

See you there.
Michael

PART 1

Next Normal Leadership

How to adapt yourself as a leader to
meet these new challenges

The Three Phases

There have been three distinct phases since the beginning of the pandemic in March 2020.

The first phase was akin to a street fight. Organizations had to react hard and fast to survive.

When it became global knowledge that widespread lockdowns were going to be a reality, companies had to make unprecedented decisions in a matter of days. Forecasting was not possible with the limited information available.

Companies were in a fight for their life, they had to get the first punch in just to make it to the next round.

For some, this was the end. Many companies went out of business. Some had to close their doors for a time, while others were forced to lay off or furlough a significant proportion of their staff.

Apart from key workers, the population was encouraged to work from home. Countries closed and working environments shifted from the shared environment of office spaces to individual houses, flats and residential areas.

Connections could only be made online.

Once the primary decisions had been made and executed, the inevitability of a protracted lockdown spanning months, as opposed to mere weeks, followed.

This catapulted us into phase 2, The Sprint.

You give it all you've got in a sprint. It's a rapid burst of extreme energy to cover the short distance to the finish line to end the race - to win.

Companies were pivoting, changing service & product mixes, and grasping to formulate some sort of plan to get us to where we envisioned the finish line was.

Back then we thought - or hoped - that this would all be over by July. The world would reopen, services would resume, and we could go back to work, go back to 'normal'.

Ah, how naive we were.

This hope has long since faded. The new reality is ever-changing, and the concept of "normal" is being redefined all the time.

This leads into the third and present stage - The Marathon.

PRINCIPLE 1:
You can't sprint a marathon.

This is a phase of endurance supported by a long-term strategy.

Our "next normal" is not looking temporary. It is stretching beyond the few months initially anticipated, the finish line is not a set point anymore, and we need to pace ourselves to reach our restated business goals.

Just like when you run a marathon, strategy, focus, and pace are essential. You have to reflect on where you are now, where you are going and what you need to do to get there.

People who are still treating this like a sprint are burning out.

The parameters of the working day have shifted unrecognizably in the necessary move to work from home.

A study from Business Insider revealed that 68% of tech workers felt more burnt out working from home than when in an office environment. We may have eliminated the tedious work commute, with its sweaty subway joys, but new stressors like extended hours, a shift in work-life-balance and video-chat-fatigue have been added.

There is also the omnipresent stress of needing to adapt to massive change consistently - not only as individuals but as teams and companies too.

Remote working is here to stay, at least in some form, for most folks. Developments in the pandemic change weekly, but the US elections are now in the rear-view mirror, with Brexit soon to follow. It's time for us to settle in and devise a plan for the long run.

I wrote this book with leaders of a post-pandemic world in mind. In these pages, you will find the toolkit that you will need to set yourself, your team and your company up for long-term success.

Being of Service

John Wooden, the legendary UCLA college men's basketball coach who won 10 national championships in a 12 year period, famously never talked about winning or losing. He taught his players how to be good people and good players.

He figured if he treated his players as young men instead of kids, have them focus on playing hard and playing smart, then more often than not they would win. He sure was right.

I've learned that great business leaders are a lot like Coach Wooden. While they are all competitors, they focus on doing whatever they can to support and be of service to their team. This means listening, understanding, and having that genuine empathy.

I meet managers who come to me saying that their team doesn't respect them. They believe that just because they are the boss and have a title that they should be automatically respected.

That's not been my experience on how respect comes about. Respect is earned through your own actions and how you treat others.

The leaders that gain that respect and loyalty from their team are leaders that are in "service" to their people. They take the view that their role is to empower and support their team. This is where the term "servant leadership" comes from. It's the "upside-down organizational chart" where the CEO is on the bottom. They are there to make sure everyone else has what they need to perform at their best.

I had another boss that said "I don't focus on the customer. I focus on the employee. If they are happy and focused, they will take great care of the customer."

Almost everyone that works for you wants to do their best. When people get frustrated - like when they feel that you don't trust them, there are too many restrictive procedures, you're unclear in your expectations, or you don't empower them - they don't see the point of putting all that effort into the job, and they resent you.

Real engagement and performance arrives when your team members know that you care about them, and you actively make decisions to support them.

The more you can shift into being a leader that genuinely cares about your team as individual people, the more successful you are going to be as a leader.

Make no mistake, this isn't about being "soft". It's about being clear what you expect out of others and from yourself; communicating that, rewarding that, and addressing when it doesn't happen.

When people don't live up to my expectations, I jump on it quickly. I get that person in, and we look at the expectation - was it clear? Was it realistic? Why did it not get met? Then we look at their effort and their process. I take into account their track record. If someone had clear objectives but didn't put the right effort into it, or has had this issue a few times before, and if they don't have the attitude or desire to change, then that person probably shouldn't be on my team or in my organization.

Each and every day, think about how you can help a member of your team. Consider how you could complement them, empower them and get them motivated. Be mindful of how you deliver criticism, keep it constructive and positive.

I believe it's up to us as leaders to create a culture and team of high-performers. If people join your team and are committed to working hard for you, then you commit to being an exceptional leader. Everyone wins.

Fostering Positivity

I've recently earned my Certificate in Neuroscience. One phrase will stick with me forever: "Neurons that wire together fire together."

That basically means that what you do will stay with you. If you watch a lot of negative press or media, you'll create negative neural pathways in your mind. If you read and focus on the positive and inspirational content, you'll reinforce that positive mindset and outlook.

This directly extends to your leadership abilities and how you relate to your team. Think about how you interact with other people in your organization. How often do you promote what is working well, or praise people that are doing things the right way?

It's easy to be the critic all the time, but what people respond to is positive reinforcement. Many leaders fall into the trap of believing this sort of management is being "soft".

They would be incorrect.

If your team is running around terrified of making mistakes and struggling with their self-esteem, they will never take risks or initiative. Teams like that aren't very effective.

As Ken Blanchard, OG Leadership Expert says, "Catch someone doing something RIGHT."

If you want a high performing team, then you need to build up the confidence, self-esteem, and skill set of each person in that team. What you'll end up with is a group of empowered people who attack change, jump on the initiative, and consistently perform miracles.

You are a Mirror

There's no secret here – any team is a reflection of the leader.

You can't tell your team what you want them to do, or how they should be if you aren't also modelling that behaviour. If you aren't practising what you preach, you will be out of alignment with your team.

This is when a team loses trust in their leader.

CASE STUDY

A few years ago, a company contacted me to run their yearly strategy session. As we were getting started, I told the CEO, Ryan, that I wanted to review a few of the documents that they had sent me prior to the meeting.

One of their values was "tight," although I didn't know what they meant by that, so I asked. Ryan replied that he wanted everybody to be tight with their agreements; everybody should be on time, they should be prepared for all meetings and honor any commitment or promise that they make.

I asked him if he was "tight" with his commitments and accountabilities. He said that of course he was. Then I reminded him that not only had he missed our last scheduled call, he had also been late for the previous one.

I repeated my original question. This time, with an embarrassed grin, he admitted that he wasn't in line with this value, even though he wanted his team to embody it.

If you've asked your team to behave in a certain way and you then flaunt these rules, it creates separation and misalignment. You have to hold yourself accountable, and to a higher level than you would expect from your employees.

As a leader, anything you do or say will be magnified. You have to be hyper-aware of how you are presenting yourself. This applies any time you are in front of your team, be it a call, a video conference, a meeting or even via email.

Ego vs Authentic Self

Your consciousness can be divided into two parts; the ego and the authentic self.

The ego's purpose is to protect you. It strives for comfort, control, and security. The ego is driven by fear, and we are fundamentally wired to protect ourselves. That means, left unchecked, you can easily shift into an ego-based state.

The ego is not necessarily a bad thing, but it can become overdeveloped and often people are driven by the ego.

On the other side of our consciousness, we have the authentic self. This is driven from a place of creativity, safety, and love. (Yes, I do use the word love when talking about leadership...)

Think about the times when you had your greatest inspiration. They will have been the times when you've been in your authentic self state. Many people tell me that they have found that creative spark from the shower (which is by nature a very safe place), or maybe on a long drive, or on vacation. All of these examples are situations where the individual would have been able to let go of everyday stress. When we let go of this stress, we can enter a peaceful state that enables us to connect to our internal authentic selves.

Poor leadership is born out of people driven by their ego.

Think of leaders that you've looked up to and respected in your life. More often than not, these individuals have a quiet confidence about them. They know themselves. They might have pushed you, but from a positive place so you would grow and learn.

Strong leaders know when to give someone a talking to, and when to place a reassuring hand on the shoulder.

They are connected to and believe in themselves. From this place of confidence and security, they can fully believe in you and the team. They receive respect and loyalty in return.

I often say that my role is to help leaders move from their ego state into their authentic self.

We can be in only one of these states at any given time; you're either able to protect yourself or create. Sometimes just having this awareness enables us to shift out of the ego and into the authentic self.

Before going into your next phone call or meeting, take a few moments to ask yourself if you are coming from a place of stress, anxiety and fear or from a place of calmness and connection. If it's the former, then stop and take a breath. Take the time to change your mindset so that you're ready, it'll be more beneficial for everyone involved.

With all this change and craziness going on around us, it's a natural instinct for our ego to dominate. However, it's even more important that you show up in your calm, authentic self right now. Your team is going to see and sense that behaviour in you, and they're going to take your lead.

Remember, you are a mirror, and you must be modelling the behaviour you want to see reflected in your team.

It's not always easy, not even necessarily fair, but it's a simple truth and how human behaviour works. This is what you signed up for. This is leadership.

Authenticity, Vulnerability & Optimism

How can you be authentic and vulnerable while still staying positive?

This is one of the most frequently asked questions from leaders. It is crucial that you get this right when addressing your team.

Leaders want to be transparent and tell the truth, but they worry that their team will get demotivated by the facts of a difficult situation.

Start with honesty and transparency. Don't hold back, deliver it straight and to the point and as accurately as possible. Make sure your energy is neutral; you mustn't sound defeated or negative when delivering this.

When you've laid out the current situation, talk about the plan of action moving forward. Let your team see the resilience and determination in your eyes. Bring your confident self. Don't get caught up talking about where things are at now - spend the rest of the time talking about the future.

Even if you don't have a well thought out plan, paint broad strokes. This particularly applies to a crisis, when you may not have a full strategy in place yet. Keep things high-level, as you don't want to give more information than you need, and then have to reverse on it later.

You want to give your team HOPE and CONFIDENCE. Hope that there's a way out, and confidence that you are the leader that will get them there.

CASE STUDY

I was working with a CEO who had renowned growth in his e-commerce organization. His whole industry was going through a major downturn. In response to this crisis, he was planning an all-employee meeting where he would address the entire company.

We were touching base, and I asked what he was thinking of telling them. He was going to reassure them that everything was fine. I studied him for a moment and then asked, "Is everything fine?" Everything was most definitely not fine.

He was facing major cutbacks across the entire company and potential layoffs if the situation continued. It couldn't be further from fine. I continued to probe him and asked if the employees were aware of what was going on. He told me that the state of the industry was common knowledge, all of his employees would be aware that things were unstable and troubling.

Had this leader failed to address the issues directly, the likelihood is that his staff would have lost faith in him. How can you expect people to trust you if you're not being honest with them?

However, we worked together to help him address the situation. We formulated a plan to broach the gravitas of what the company was facing.

When it came to the day of the company-wide meeting, the CEO was well prepared. He stood up in front of everybody, and said that they had had a good run for the past 10 years, and he was so proud of everyone. He was sincere and upfront - he told them that the industry was hitting a tough time, that they weren't forecasting any revenue growth and the company would struggle to even make a profit.

There was a collective sigh of relief throughout the crowd.

Their leader had addressed the elephant in the room and gained their respect in one fell swoop.

He went on to say that his goal was to get through the difficult period without letting anyone go, but that this was not something he could guarantee. He said he would need the help and support of his teams to do this.

The organization rallied around him.

The accounting team ditched their plans of getting a new department, one lady offered to cut her hours in half so she could take care of her new grandchild, and the offers came flooding in from all areas of the company.

The devastating blow that he had been building up in his head and trying to work out ways to shield them all from, actually wound up bringing them closer together. The company not only survived the downturn without having to let anyone go, but they ended up acquiring two other companies. They made the difficult decisions early on and as a team, rather than waiting until it was too late to do anything.

This "high-growth" CEO achieved because he addressed the issue head-on, he had a strategy, he gave everybody a purpose and something to respond to - an action plan to fight the problem.

This is a display of "unwavering pragmatic optimism". Unwavering because people will pick up on and cling to the smallest piece of doubt. Pragmatic because you have to be authentic and practical. And of course, optimism because you're giving people hope.

You have got to have honest talks about the difficult times. Make sure your energy and mindset are rock-solid at the point of delivery.

Think about the outward projection of your mood. If you are harbouring stress or negative energy, and bring this to a team meeting, you will share that energy. Moods are contagious. It's ok to have a bad day, or show that you're stressed, you are human too. Just be mindful of how much you are projecting on to your team.

If you're struggling with this, consider working with a coach. Go to tiny.cc/nextnormal-coaching to learn more about how my team and I can help you in this. Working with a professional can give you the tools, space, and support to get back to the positive, healthy, strong leader your team needs.

Resilience

Resilience is a crucial topic that leaders are requesting help with in the current climate. When you build resilience into your team, they can handle whatever comes up.

Nine key factors can be taught to individuals and reinforced through conversations, coaching, meetings, and any other times you see fit.

1. **Learn from every setback**. While this can sound trite and basic, it can also be a game-changer; with every setback, figure out what you've learned and how you're going to change your approach next time. This creates a positive even when things didn't turn out as planned.

2. **Focus on the positives & celebrate every win**. Positive momentum builds positive results. Track and celebrate each and every victory.

3. **Keep your eye on the goal.** The setbacks don't matter if you reach your desired destination in the end, they can even be character building. If you achieve your goals and are fulfilling your purpose, failures and setbacks get forgotten very quickly.

4. **Laugh it off.** The more humour and lightheartedness you can bring to a setback, the easier it is to get through it. Humor can quickly dissipate negative feelings and re-engage people. Remember this when someone seems defeated; though bear in mind that tact is required.

5. **Grieve and then move on.** It's ok to get frustrated and even angry when things don't go well. Give yourself the time you need to process those emotions, then let it go.

6. **Remind yourself of your own success stories.** Revisit all the times you've actually succeeded because those are the times that really matter. A quick resilience hack is to do a "50 stack". When you're feeling a bit sorry for yourself, take a pile of 50 note cards and write down 50 times that you've succeeded. Once you see them all stacked up, you'll realize how powerful you really are.

7. **Get a pep talk.** This may be the American in me talking, but calling a friend, letting them know you're feeling a bit beaten up, and having them remind you how amazing you are can work really well.

8. **Exercise.** When you exercise, your body is releasing endorphins, and you'll naturally shift into a better mood.

9. **Take a Break.** Instead of jumping right into things when you're feeling a bit stuck, take 15 minutes, an hour, or a day, to do other activities. When you get back to it, you'll be seeing things with different eyes.

Communication

It's imperative to choose your words carefully and communicate a consistent message.

You need to keep the team involved in the company's purpose and strategy. You can do this by reaffirming both in weekly or monthly meetings. Just make sure you're not being boring, too dry, or repetitive - keeping people involved means that they stay engaged.

Make sure that you are approachable and your team knows you are open to answering questions. Perhaps a few times a month make yourself available to answer questions around team performance and what's happening in the wider company. This will improve engagement, loyalty, and retention.

Be wary of idle gossip, or even thinking out loud within earshot of members of staff...

When I was running one of my companies in San Diego, California, I went out to lunch with one of my friends. He was telling me about the abundance of opportunities 2 hours north up the I-5 Interstate in Los Angeles. We discussed opening an office there to take advantage of all the potential business. As I walked through the lobby back into the building, I casually mentioned to our office manager how interesting it could be to have an office in LA.

30 minutes later my lead programmer came in to talk to me, she had heard we would be opening an office in Los Angeles, and she wanted to let me know that she would be open to relocating.

Within half an hour, an offhand comment from me had been transformed into a full-fledged rumor, with members of staff declaring their preference of office location and desire to move.

Then and there I learned that I had to be so careful with my words, who I said them to, and where I said them. As a leader, people look to you with different eyes, you have an authority that other members of staff don't. An off-the-cuff comment from you can be taken as gospel and spread around the office like wildfire.

In highly charged times of stress, change and disarray, it's more likely that your words will be taken out of context, reappropriated and misunderstood.

There is a climate of general hysteria in these times. A flippant comment from you about cuts backs on office space could be taken wildly out of context. Before you know it they'll be rumors of layoffs and a permanent move to working from home because the company can't afford the office space.

Even if this is the case, you don't want an office rumor to be the way this sensitive information is delivered. The last thing you need is confusion and hysteria working against you.

With the first lockdown in March, some CEO's chose to address their team every single day. This was happening in large companies too, with tens of thousands of employees listening to the message and asking questions in response.

The more background chat that is going on, the more frequently your teams need to hear from you - even if the message contains no new news. This reassurance will keep conspiracy theories from circulating and will be a reminder that you are in control and on their side.

I'm a big believer in frequent, shorter, communication bulletins as opposed to saving the information up and having infrequent, long sessions.

Even if you don't have the specifics sorted out, you need to be focusing on moving forward. Let your team know you are working on the details, and aim to get them on board and involved in creating the solution.

People need hope. With hope comes confidence and trust in you and your leadership that there is a way out.

Support Network

A t our cores, we are social creatures with an underlying evolutionary pack mentally. We like to be with other people. Who we have around us can really affect our mood and how we behave.

Who in your life do you have that you can share it all with? Who is that positive influence that uplifts you when it all gets a bit much? Is there someone who brings you down, a toxic influence that might be making things a little bit harder?

Take a look at your support network, those people you surround yourself with, and increase the positive influences, decrease the negative if you can - nobody has time for that sort of toxicity.

Your support network should consist of 3 main branches formed from your social life.

The first is family. This could be a partner, a sibling, a parent, or someone you've known a long time that you consider to be a family member.

The second branch is friendship. This consists of people in your life that are not colleagues or family members - someone neutral you can grumble to about the other branches of your network.

The third is the people you work with that are your trusted allies. Work friends that fulfil the professional branch of your support network.

You need to cultivate these relationships, and preferably have more than one person in each area. Life is hard, and we all need to vent or have someone to lean on and have fun with.

Having different relationships in other areas of your life allows freedom from each branch. Your support bases will be covered. If you find one base lacking, don't fret, one or two solid relationships can be as valuable, if not more, than ten weak ones.

Outside Support

If reflecting on your support network has made you feel anxious, if it all seems impossibly difficult, or you think you are lacking a good support network, I would recommend reaching out to a professional.

My leadership abilities really took off when I first started working with coaches. I currently utilize several coaches across different areas of my life. When you employ a skilled professional whose sole job is focused on helping you move forward, you really have no choice but to do just that. That's a whole lot of focused energy and skill directed at progressing your development.

During challenging times, leaders need new skills, support and a calm head to help them to make the vast array of decisions on their plate. That's a lot for one person to deal with without some sort of sounding board.

A formal group of peers can also give you support, accountability, and growth. These are often called mastermind groups. These groups tend to meet regularly with other people that are in a similar situation and/or have similar goals.

Individual coaching is best when you want focused attention and one-on-one support. This is ideal if you're dealing with issues and topics that you may not like to share with others, or you want to make swift progress. Masterminds and group coaching give you the power and diversity of a group, although good chemistry between group members is pivotal to its success.

I work with a few coaches myself (each one focusing on an area of my life I want to grow and succeed in) and am a member of two mastermind peer groups. I also work with select leaders in one-on-one mentoring and coaching engagement and run masterminds where people can learn and get support as leaders.

If you're interested in exploring working with me directly, and to see what masterminds and training I currently have planned, follow this link: tiny.cc/nextnormal-coaching

PART 2

Team Mental & Emotional Health

Learn how you can create and maintain a healthy, resilient, and engaged team, even in times of unprecedented change.

Your first job as a leader is to make sure your team is healthy and strong. When my team knows that I'm genuinely focusing on making life better for them, the return in loyalty, respect, and performance is outstanding.

People are still reeling from the massive change and disruption that came with the pandemic. There's so much uncertainty through all walks of life right now. You can bet that it is affecting the stress levels, if not the mental health, of your team.

A piece of advice I give leaders right off the bat is that they have to spend significantly more time managing and leading their people right now.

It's going to take your focus and personal attention to get your team to where they need to be.

People have been running on adrenaline for way too long and are now paying the price.

Cracks are Showing

After collating my survey results and considering the many conversations I've been having with both managers and individual contributors, it's clear that people are at their breaking point.

If you don't make changes quickly, it's going to lead to long-term issues with your people, your culture, and overall performance.

In the study conducted by my team and I, 75% of senior leaders said that their overall mental and emotional health is worse off than pre-pandemic levels. Of this, 25% say that their mental and emotional health is at a dangerously low level.

Statistically, 3 in 4 of your senior leadership team are not doing well, and 1 in 4 are severely suffering right now.

Taking all levels of an organization into account, a whopping 60% of the workforce are doing worse mentally and emotionally than in pre-pandemic life.

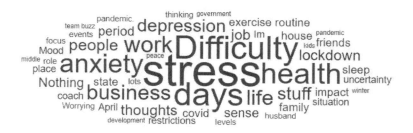

The illustration is a "word cloud" that depicts the response of survey participants' reactions to the current climate. The larger the word, the more often it was mentioned.

It looks like we have some work to do.

PRINCIPLE 2:
You don't find out about mental health
Issues until it's too late.

Once you find out that people are suffering from significant mental health issues, like clinical depression, problems with anxiety, or something similar, it's a serious issue with no quick solution.

Mental health doesn't just affect the individual, it can impact on family life too. It can also send shockwaves through the team that they work with, and even the broader organization.

It's our job and responsibility as leaders to do what we can to prevent and support this.

Empathy

Empathy is a valuable skill you need to cultivate as a leader.

Empathy is an easy concept to talk about in theory, but it takes a deft touch and experience to figure out how to master it as a leader. Leadership empathy can be seen through caring about people in your team; it's about knowing what's going on in their lives and how they're feeling about it.

Empathy is about taking all of this on board and then caring enough to work with the person to create better conditions.

How this is done drifts into the "art" of leadership rather than the science.

Once you understand what empathy is, and how to incorporate it to your management style, you will see a difference in the response of your people.

Empathetic leadership generates loyalty and drives up team performance. People like to know they are supported and cared about, it makes them feel valued.

PRINCIPLE 3:
Care about the person and they'll
care about their job.

CASE STUDY

I work with a managing director who has already implemented much of what I've covered in this book. His team has responded positively as he really cares about them.

Recently, I checked in to see how he was doing. From his hesitation, I could tell he was having a tough time.

He reports periodically to the owner of the company and is, for the most part, left to his own devices to run the business. The owner has never shown interest in the welfare of the people on the ground. He has only ever been concerned with the financial performance of the business.

This MD was giving so much to his staff that he burnt out. He needed a break and told the owner he was having a hard time, and then took two weeks of holiday to recharge.

He made himself vulnerable in an open conversation to the owner about his physical and mental state. Despite this, the owner never followed up to see how he was doing.

All this MD wanted was some sort of vested personal interest from the owner. An "Are you feeling better after your break?" would have been enough; something human to connect to, so he would feel less like a machine churning out figures.

The lack of connection, humanity, and interest from his boss was the last straw. That was his last week at the company, he resigned.

I can't blame him.

This mirrors a Qualtrics survey from April 2020.

67% of people show a higher level of stress than before the pandemic.

60% do not feel supported by their manager.

56% do not feel comfortable bringing up that perceived lack of support to their manager.

What would happen if you ran the same poll in your company? How can you avoid this level of negativity and mistrust within your team?

PRINCIPLE 4:
Leadership is personal now.

Your role is to lead. This position changes the personal/professional balance between you and your team.

Before this year, with the collision of the home and workspace, I would have said some professional and emotional distance between you and your team was healthy and necessary.

2020 has changed all that. We're dealing with health threats, lockdowns, tiers, different rules for different parts of the country, and working from home with kids and relatives running around. We've been confined to socialising with our household, isolated from other people and our usual way of working. On top of that, office dynamics have moved to a virtual space, and we need to get to grips with all the change and adjustment that this means.

You need to bridge the gap, check in with your team and find out what's going on for people in their personal lives. Hopefully, they are taking all this in their stride and finding the balance between home, work and new team dynamics. However, they could be living a nightmare trying to keep their head above the water, juggling home and work at the same time.

How can you support your team?

It's all about taking the time to really care for your teammates as individual people. Now I'm not talking about adding them on LinkedIn or Facebook and liking the pictures they post of their weekend lockdown antics. Caring is going to require you to use the tools of a leader and as an empathetic human to make that connection.

The good news is that it's totally free. It's going to take a little of your time, and you need to tap into your humanity.

Take a few moments and objectively reflect on how you are treating your staff;

» Are you there for them?

» Are you reading in between the lines?

» Are you taking the time in one-to-one conversations to find out who they are and how they are doing?

» Are you listening to your own intuition?

» Are you asking yourself the question "what does my team need from me?"

The more you start taking the time to slow down and ask yourself these questions, the easier this process becomes. Before long, these will be unconscious compassionate actions that you apply to both your professional and personal relationships. (How to be a better human 101.)

People often say more in what they don't say.

It's up to you to get to know your teammates as individual people. You need to take notice and pay attention to the nuances of different characters.

When you get to know someone then you can see beyond the outward projection they show to the world, and hear what they're really saying.

Warning Signs

Y ou don't have to become a mind reader to be able to predict the mental and emotional health of your team members.

They will display characteristic warning signs in deviations from their normal behaviour.

If you have a team member who has always sent you emails at 2 AM, that's not an issue. However, if you have a team member who has generally worked within regular business hours, and you start noticing emails sent in the middle of the night, there's cause for concern.

Below is a list of potential behavioural areas that you can use to compare pre and post-pandemic actions. A discernible shift in demeanour may indicate deeper issues that need to be addressed.

Meetings:
» Misses or is habitually late for

» Always on mute or have their camera off

» Withdrawing or not participating

» Focusing on negatives

» Becoming defensive and argumentative

Communication:
» Receiving comms from them at strange hours

» Not clear or unprofessional communications

» Missed messages or non-timely responses

ions:

» Looking disheveled / not showering / not professional

» Taking sick days / headaches / stomach issues

» Decreased performance

» More complaints and grievances

» Work / sleep patterns changed

Emotional:

» Twitchy or nervous

» Mood swings

» Loss of motivation, commitment and confidence

» Increased emotional reactions – being more tearful, sensitive or aggressive

» Each deviation could be a clue to something, but the one-off incident shouldn't set off alarm bells.

» Repeated occurrences, or a shift in behaviour across the board, does point to something deeper going on that needs to be addressed.

Socially Connecting

Every leader who has a healthy, performing, engaged team has implemented non-work, social networking opportunities into their team's regular schedules.

CASE STUDY

A software company manager allotted a few time slots every day, so people had the opportunity to chat about non-work subjects. I was surprised at this as he had a team of 7, and it sounded like a lot of time for a relatively small group.

However, they had always been a social team. Ordinarily, they would eat lunch together at the office, chat on coffee breaks and enjoy "after work" drinks at the pub. All of these impromptu get-togethers had been taken out with the pandemic.

The manager accounted for the time spent socializing through the working day pre-pandemic; his new allotted social slots weren't taking up any more time than the unscheduled chatting they would have done before the pandemic.

It worked - the online chatting incentive had been really well received and kept his team together through remote working.

He has also been able to use this system to notice "red flags" that might have gone unnoticed in isolation. If he sees that somebody hasn't been in one of these sessions for a few days, he gets in touch directly with the individual to check that there isn't something else going on.

Leaders are trying all sorts of virtual activities to keep the team vibe going. Different things work for different teams, some have daily ventures - others prefer a weekly or monthly get-together.

Quiz nights were very popular with lockdown round one - others found their general knowledge exhausted with lockdown round two, and the whole quiz thing flopped. Just having space for free-flowing non-work chat worked for some teams.

Try things out, listen for feedback and then adjust. Put someone else in charge - nominate a social secretary and rotate that responsibility. This can energize your team without putting too much pressure on one person. It brings in fresh ideas and makes it less of a "top-down" event.

Exercise challenges can be an excellent thing for people to get involved with. However, you have to be aware of excluding people that may not be in shape or people with disabilities.

There have been step-counting challenges where you, as a group, set goals - the collaborative teams daily step count all contributes to the total. This could encourage your staff to get out and go for a lunchtime walk without making it seem like a chore. You can incorporate prizes for this as well, make it fun.

Another activity to consider is in-office online yoga. Float the idea to your team and see who might be interested. You can speak to a yoga teacher about providing private online classes for your team. A good yoga teacher will be more than happy to come up with a program for you that can fit the schedule, abilities and needs of your team.

It can be a great bonding experience and gives people something non-work related to talk about and share... without the awkward moment of actually having to see your boss in downward facing dog.

Avoiding Burnout

Real Burnout is a serious medical condition with potentially chronic consequences. It's high on the list of leaders' concerns right now.

Make yourself aware of the symptoms so you can notice the early warning signs in your team members and in yourself. Early prevention is vital, and the condition is reversible if addressed quickly.

Burnout does not discriminate. It can affect anyone at any age, industry, and title.

A person with burnout will suffer mental, emotional and/or physical exhaustion as the result of long-term stress.

Many symptoms define this condition, but general ones to look out for include lower resistance to illness, a pessimistic outlook, exhaustion, demotivation and detachment at work and in personal relationships, alongside a lower level of productivity.

This condition doesn't suddenly appear. It's not like a virus or a rash, and it doesn't show up on a blood test. It tends to build gradually over time with 5 progressive stages.

Phase 1 "The Sweet Spot":

» Manageable, where we want people to stay

» Experiencing the anticipated stress of the job

» Sustained energy levels

» Job satisfaction, accepting responsibility, optimistic mindset

» Creativity, high productivity

Phase 2 "The Slip":

»   Some days feel harder than others

»   Job dissatisfaction, irritability, inability to focus

»   High blood pressure, palpitations, fatigue

»   Withdrawn, self-neglect, sleep disturbances

Phase 3 "The Scale Tips":

»   Chronic Stress

»   Lack of hobbies or enjoyment in life

»   Missed work deadlines, repeated tardiness, procrastination

»   Apathy, aggressive outbursts, persistent fatigue - especially in the morning

»   Reliance on substances like caffeine/drugs/alcohol

Phase 4 "Critical":

»   Intervention - clinical or psychological support may be needed

»   Chronic headaches, chronic stomach or bowel issues

»   Behavioural changes, pessimistic outlook

»   Obsess over problems, desire to isolate

»   Total neglect of personal needs

Phase 5 "Habitual Burnout"

»   Symptoms of burnout become ingrained

»   Significant physical or emotional health issue

»   Medical, psychological and functional support needed

»   Long road to recovery, a full recovery may not be possible

Here are five things you can do to avoid burnout for your team (and yourself);

Set Clear Boundaries

There are times when you want to crack on and focus on work. There are also times when you need to turn away, connect with something you enjoy, and rest up. One of the hardest things with working from home is that the boundaries between home life and work-life become blurred.

The balance tends to swing in favour of working more.It can begin to feel like every waking hour is overshadowed by the ever-present workload.

Coach your staff to have defined hours for work and non-work (You can keep this the same time-wide or it can vary from person to person).

Some firms are actually shutting off email sending on the IT server-side after a specific time. This means that any emails sent after, say, 6 PM will get queued until 6 AM the next day and released then.

Enforce Time Off

The temptation has been to neglect annual leave this year.

Everyone has been stuck at home, unable to leave the country, and as a result, have not been taking time off.

Firms include holiday days in their contracts for a reason; you have got to give your brain and body a break from working all the time. Everyone needs that time to recharge and detach.

Many bosses have resorted to ordering their employees to take time off this year so that people wouldn't burn out.

Make sure that you and your staff are taking time off totally away from the virtual office; no emails, work responsibilities, text messages or calendar invites.

With a decent break, people can come back with a new life infused into them.

Connect to a Purpose

Working just to get paid isn't inspiring. When people know they are working towards a goal that is more significant than just showing up to work to get the paycheck, they get energized.

Think about any passion project you may have worked on. How did you feel? I'm betting that you experienced engagement and energy irrespective of the monetary outcome.

Having a purpose is integral to motivation.

Almost everyone has personal goals and dreams that drive them. In later sections, we will discuss how to come up with a team and company purpose too.

A great leader knows what drives each one of their team members. Maybe an individual wants to send their kid to one of the best universities, or buy a summer house with their partner, they may want to work with a charity, or even retire early.

If you can connect what they do every day in the office to what their life goals are, they will see that working in your team is worth more than just the paycheck.

Focus and Simplicity

The road to burn out is disorientating, people lose their sense of prioritization and time management.

Get together with your team member that is struggling, look at their workload, and take anything you can off of their to-do list. Focus on what really needs to get done.

Take a look at the management of this to-do list and how they are keeping track of what they need to do. Does your company have an online space where you can post tasks? Or perhaps the person prefers to keep a journal/writing pad/post-it notes to physically write down what they need to do.

Keeping an organized system with precise tasks in view can help lower stress levels - especially when you get to cross those tasks off.

If there are any stressful projects, presentations, or meetings coming up see if you can shield them from that extra pressure. Reduce the white noise and get them engaged with the bit they need to do rather than looking at the whole project and panicking.

Work with your team member on their remaining list of things to do. Give them small, doable tasks that they can check off and get a sense of accomplishment.

Build on Positives

Positive momentum builds positive momentum.

If someone is struggling, you need to help build their confidence back up. By coaching your team member to get little things done correctly time after time, they'll start to gain their sense of self again.

Let them know that they're doing a good job if you truly believe they are, praise always needs to come from an authentic place.

These are all small things that you can include every day that can be the difference between recovery and failure.

We're not talking about major modifications on your part here, but if they lose this battle with their health, you lose too. Think of it as a short term investment that beats losing a person in the long-term.

Understanding Extroverts and Introverts

There are three personality types to contend with in every team, and each one requires a different management style. Being able to identify and adapt depending on who you're working with is a crucial skill.

Any given individual is either an introvert, an extrovert or an ambivert.

An introvert gets recharged by being quiet and alone, while an extrovert will thrive on being around people. An ambivert (2/3 of the population) is a combination of both.

Introverts may actually enjoy working in lockdown; they could be excelling in the working from home environment.

Working from home allows for more control over the environment, this induces productivity in the introvert.

There is a downside. While the introvert may be getting more work done, the leader and other teammates can forget about them in an "out of sight, out of mind" scenario. This group of people are less likely to take part in optional meetings, are less vocal on calls, and may knuckle down quietly getting their workload done behind the scenes.

There's a natural tendency for the introvert to isolate both professionally and socially. As a result, they may be dealing with issues and struggling quietly in isolation - suffering in silence as it were.

CASE STUDY

One leader I talked to told me about an introverted member of his team who, after a few weeks, started to really struggle.

Pre-pandemic, this individual was quiet and never an active participant in the office chat. However, the manager discovered he really needed to be in the office atmosphere as he thrived being around people and the office banter.

It turns out this team member lived in a tiny flat with his girl-friend. Once lockdown began, his working conditions were far from ideal. He had to work all day sitting on his bed as his partner was working in the main room. He quickly became lonely and disconnected.

You must keep tabs on the mental welfare of your team and understand the conditions that they are working in.

The polar opposite of the introvert is the extrovert.

Extroverted people are having more difficulties working from home than any other group.

These individuals flourish in the interaction with people, and can quickly become depressed when taken out of their natural social situations.

An extrovert will prefer a variety of tasks and tend to work best when bouncing ideas off other people. They'll be the ones in the room thinking "out loud". They get a kick out of the random conversations that can pop up, and can prefer these collaborations to scheduled meetings.

An extrovert may also require more validation than the introvert to keep them happy and secure in their role.

The small talk and back-to-back meetings that drain the introvert, energize the extrovert. They are also far more creative in a busy space with lots of people around.

Basically, everything that feeds an extrovert has disappeared with the pandemic.

So how to adapt to this new way of working?

We need to know who we are and what our needs are to be happier and more productive overall. We have to adapt to the situation we've found ourselves in.

I spoke to Fiona Buckley, who has a background in business and a Masters degree in Work Behaviour and Occupational Psychology. She has been providing her valuable insight to companies throughout lockdown with a series of remote webinars, "How to Win your Day, Working from Home."

I interviewed her on the complexities of managing extroverts and introverts and asked if she had any practical advice on how to work from home for your personality type.

Extroverts are needing more adaptations to work from home. They need to be focusing on "flexing" their personality where and when they can. Instead of shrinking away and making themselves miserable at home, look for how you can encourage these people to utilize their skills as extroverts virtually.

Planning back to back meetings is perfect for an extrovert, they don't need the buffer time in between calls at all. However, you do need to be aware of their schedule. On a day with one meeting, this individual is likely to over-exert and unload all their pent up personality on that call. This is a terrible dynamic for the rest of the team or whoever is on the call - they'll talk right over everyone.

On the other hand, if an introvert is on more than 3 video calls a day, it can drain their energy and mood. They need space in between meetings so they get some breathing room and can recharge.

Spur of the moment meetings aren't a thing right now, so the extrovert needs to find ways to compensate as they crave that spontaneity. Think about introducing an open forum, so they can still get that "boucibility" between people.

Extroverts are known for networking and self-promotion. They need to play up to this right now and make themselves visible.

Fiona suggests that all people, be it an introvert, extrovert or an ambivert, need to be pivoting into the fundamental skills associated with their personality type. Set yourself some goals so you can utilize and excel at these skills in the virtual space.

The more you and your team use these skills, the happier you all will be.

A Personalized Plan

I often work with leaders to create a personal plan for their team members. This includes identifying where they are on the personality scale, how they like to be communicated with, and what they need as far as support.

Everyone has a preferred way of communicating. Some people like a phone call, others prefer email, while others like to use a chat application or text message. For the personal touch and non-standard working comms (as there may be company standard for communications) meet people where they feel most comfortable.

No matter how much they prefer typed communication, you should be checking in with them on a video chat or in-person at least once a month.

External issues have a significant impact on work performance. For example, my US-based bookkeeper, who I've worked with for over a decade, started missing deadlines just after the COVID lockdown started. This was frustrating for both myself and my managing director as it was causing issues with our business.

Eventually, I was able to reach her on the phone and asked her what was going on. She told me that they had 7 kids at home, aged from 5 to 20, all in a small house. She was just trying to hang on for dear life.

After our conversation, we decided to switch bookkeepers since it wasn't working for either party. She was happy with the decision. We had a good relationship, and she wanted the best for us, she just couldn't handle the workload at the time.

Similarly, I was working with an organization that had a lot of international offices. The lady who ran the German operations had an 8-month old child and her husband had a job that required that he travel for two weeks straight each month.

Before the pandemic, they had relied on childcare during her husband's travel weeks. When lockdown hit, this was no longer an option. This has put her under an incredible amount of stress in her husband's absence.

We are working in a new world. Up until now, it may not have been necessary or even "proper" for you to understand the scope of your team's home lives.

Everything has changed.

The lines between the office and the home have been blurred. It's essential to understand what's going on in the lives of your team. From a place of understanding, you can make the appropriate arrangements, or suggestions, so that they can manage their responsibilities - and not just the ones directly related to their role.

This is the level of empathy that is required from successful leaders. It will build strong relationships with a firm foundation of loyalty and engagement. Your team will look to you as a supportive and understanding leader during this time of crisis.

Caspar Craven, a good friend and expert in building high-performance teams, recently released a book called "Be More Human: Rethinking the Rules of High-Performance Teamwork".

In one of our many walks around the Surrey (UK) countryside he shared with me this wisdom:

"We are all humans. The sooner we are honest about what is going on with us, within us, and what we could use for support, the better off we'll all be. We have to make it safe to be vulnerable, and that's a real key for building high-performance teams."

This isn't a suggestion, it is a fundamental necessity in the world we find ourselves living in. It's the right thing to do.

One-on-One's

One-on-one video calls with each member of your team are imperative right now. You may want to do these as frequently as every few days.

During times of change and difficulty, I would check-in at least every two weeks with my direct reports, and more often than that if I had time to.

A one-on-one will give you information and the access to build a connection that you just won't get in any other team meetings or via email.

PRINCIPLE 5:
Earn the right to have real conversations.

Imagine a weed in the garden. The seed is buried deep in the earth and then it sprouts. From this sprout grows one stem and then another. Before you know it, the garden is overrun with weeds. Cutting the weed at the leaf or at the stem won't solve your problem, you have to dig down to the roots to remove the cause.

We can apply this analogy to mental and physical health concerns.

There is always a root cause - symptoms don't appear without rhyme or reason. Addressing the surface problems - like behavioural changes or recurring sickness, won't solve the problem. They'll just keep coming back with a vengeance until that root cause has been found and dealt with.

Supporting someone to find their root cause takes skill and tact on your part. It could be as simple as being a sounding board for that person, so they can talk through everything that is going on and maybe even realize it for themselves.

It's much harder to communicate properly now, through the screen we lose the non-verbal queues of energy and body language. You have to make up for that and be hyper-attentive during your virtual one-to-ones.

Here is a guide for having a virtual one-on-one with someone who may be struggling and you want them to open up.

Bear in mind these calls can go one of two ways.

On the one hand, the individual will be so relieved that you have taken the time and interest to notice that they are fully ready to share with you. In which case great, you can act on that accordingly. On the other hand, they may be closed off and potentially feel uncomfortable, awkward or put on the spot, and it may take some time to get them to open up.

» **Schedule** the call when you both have time in your calendar to engage and focus on that meeting without distractions. You wouldn't have a face-to-face while you were both working on other projects, or checking your phone and emails - a virtual one-to-one should be no different. Put it all down and focus.

» **Video call** where possible.

» **Centre Yourself** before the call. Spend a few minutes to shift your mindset to where you are prepared to really listen. This will also help you to work out your strategy for the call and revisit any notes you have.

» **LISTEN.** You shouldn't be talking more than ▢ of the time. This is a place for them to share and express.

» **Clear Intention.** You're not here to talk about details of projects, clients or other work issues. You want to know how they're doing and what, if anything, you can do to support them.

» **Pause.** Give them some space to see if they are ready to open up.

» **Be Vulnerable.** If you are encountering some resistance, it can be helpful to let your guard down first. You don't have to overshare, but let them know how you've been feeling and dealing with the whole situation too. Revealing some of your own battles shows them that it's ok to admit to having a tough time.

» **Address the problem directly.** If the person is not offering any insight, tell them, with sensitivity, that you get the sense that there is something more going on with them. Let them know that you would really like to help them if it is within your power.

» **Be specific.** Share a few incidents that might have indicated to you that they have not been coping so well. For example, missed staff meetings, or a switched-off camera in calls etc.

» **The Energy** you bring to these meetings is vital to the success of their delivery. This is supposed to be a reassuring and calming catch up for your team members - not a stressful performance review.

» **Tone.** How you say it is as important as what you say. Tone of voice has a real impact on the nervous system. Sounds stimulate and tone the vagus nerve. This is the longest nerve in the body, starting at the back of the brain, running through all the organs, and finishing in the gut. It impacts the nervous system and our stress response. A more melodic tone can shift the body from the sympathetic (fight, flight or freeze) to the parasympathetic state (rest and digest). By being aware and controlling the tone of your voice, you can help calm someone down.

» **Body language** - are you sitting up straight in a comfortable position? Are you looking directly into the screen? Maintaining physical engagement will encourage mental and emotional engagement.

» **Barriers.** If you don't need to wear glasses for the call, try not to. We already have the barrier of the screen, so think about the ways you can maintain as much uninterrupted eye contact as possible.

» **Create a safe space.** You need to hold this meeting without judgement and without expectation. If the individual chooses not to share, don't shame them or voice your disappointment. They will come to you when they feel ready and safe to do so.

» **Don't interrupt** if someone starts sharing. If they pause, hold the silence even if it feels uncomfortable. It's likely they've been processing something internally. Even just airing this out with you might resolve the problem, you may not need to action it at all.

» **Support** them as a person and as their boss. If the problem is out of your depth or you're not sure how to answer, thank them for sharing with you. You need to let them know that you've heard them. Don't be afraid to ask them how you can help or ask what they need from you.

If neither of you are sure what you can do in terms of support, tell the person that you are going to give the matter some thought, and that they should too.

Pencil in another meeting in the next few days to give you both some time to go away, maybe do some research, talk to Human Resources, or just reflect on it. You can then return with a well thought out plan of action that will help. This takes some of the pressure off of you so you don't have to address everything right on the spot. It's ok to not have all the answers.

You need to see calls and connections like this as an investment.

If you want to create a healthy, high-performance remote team, you need to stay connected to each and every person in your group.

After all, how do you think you earn respect and build loyalty?

People will only follow you if they believe in you and are connected to you as a person. Now that you're not all in the office, you have to invest time into activities that cultivate this.

If you're thinking that all this is a real shift and an entirely different way of working, you're not alone. Like any change, these are new mindsets, skills, and habits that you have to learn.

Take it from me, I've been working and leading remotely for over 20 years - it didn't happen overnight. It took a long time, but I built up the skills that I'm sharing with you now. They are tried and testing, they will make you and your team stronger and more effective - to the company and to each other.

All of this can be a lot. You may be thinking that your organization may need my help. If so, go to www.RMichaelAnderson.com to learn about the training, support, and coaching options my team and I offer.

PART 3

Virtual Team Performance

Driving team performance with a remote
or hybrid workforce.

Now that you've addressed the immediate health needs of your team, you can focus on driving performance.

Part two will discuss leadership and management strategies and tactics that have been adapted for virtual teams.

A properly structured and supported virtual or hybrid* team can be as, if not more, productive than a fully in-office team.

(*Note: When you see the word hybrid in this book I'm using it to refer to a working model that has both in-office workers and remote workers. This can consist of a fully remote team, or a staggered re-entry with people working different days in the office, or coming into the office for meetings or get-togethers.)

Motivation & Inspiration

During times of change, and especially in lockdown situations, people need motivation and inspiration more than ever.

The difference between people burning out and everyone being fully engaged is often down to your ability to motivate and inspire them.

You don't have to be a "rah-rah" cheerleader, but you do need to put effort into keeping people energized. With limited travel, sports, restaurants and other restrictions, many people have had their "fun" activities taken out of their lives.

We've had a year of just work and just family. That's intense, especially when all the "fun time" opportunities have been so radically reduced. There hasn't been any buffer time to recharge and reset.

As a result, work has taken centre stage for a lot of people and overlapped into areas of life that were once work free. You can make sure that work is something that gives them, rather than drains, energy.

Individual Purpose

Understanding the individual motivations and purpose of each team member is key to collective motivation.

You need to discover each person's motivation through day-to-day communication and in the review process. Find out what drives them; it may be developing new skills, reaching new levels within their career, or receiving praise in front of their peers.

When you find out what drives an individual and what they really want from their job, you can use that as an incentive to motivate them further. Once you find it out, add that into their personal plan.

What works for one person doesn't necessarily work for another. You need to tailor your approach. This can be a powerful methodology that instigates loyalty and increases engagement within your team.

Team Purpose & Goals

People like to contribute to a winning team.

Use your creativity to find a larger goal that people can rally behind to make progress towards.

A team purpose (or goal in this case) can come in many different forms:

- » **Financial** goals could be achieving a certain amount of revenue, profit, or savings

- » **Achievement** goals could be successfully integrating a new software package, launching a new product

- » **Outside** goals could include raising a certain amount of money for a good cause, charity work, supporting your local community, or social causes.

Here are guidelines to keep in mind to get the most out of your goal setting;

- » **Doable.** It has to be achievable, yet it will stretch people a little bit to get there. Too ambitious and it will drain energy, too easy, and it will not provide a sense of accomplishment.

- » **Duration.** Ideally, it will last a few weeks or months with a specific end date in the medium-term future. If it's longer than that, create milestones to celebrate.

- » **Reward.** If your goal is financial (make *x* amount of profit), then you want your rewards to be financial too (profit or gift certificates). After all, it's no fun making someone else more money if all you get is a pat on the back. Be careful with too many financial goals like this, if it becomes regular people begin to expect them as part of their compensation.

- » **Delegate.** In some cases, the team can define the exact goal and reward (with the go-ahead from the leader of course).

This gives them ownership and creates less work for you. You can also put someone else in charge of leading and monitoring the initiative.

» **Make it FUN.** Find ways to inject excitement into it. Give the project a name - a FUN name. When they reach a milestone, you could send everyone a novelty gift to their house (something small like a badge or a hat).

» **Renegotiate.** Don't be afraid to redefine the terms, nothing is set in stone. If something comes up and the goal looks out of reach, then adjust it to make it doable. If it seems too easy, don't change the original goal or reward, instead, add a stretch goal with an additional prize.

» **Track** it regularly. Make sure people see the progress they are making towards the goal on at least a weekly basis.

» **Stay involved.** Make sure you know what's going on with the project. Send personal notes and give public recognition to those engaged with the project and so forth.

When I was running my main software company, we did things like this all the time.

I would have so many other priorities to do that sometimes I would see this as a distraction to other, more important, tasks. Despite that, I would almost always make time to stay engaged, and it paid long-term dividends in a big way.

The team would get so much fun and benefit out of it, they were a much higher performing team because of these initiatives.

Team & Company Purpose

Many companies have a purpose and vision alongside strategic goals.

In larger teams, divisions and workgroups may have their own independent purpose too. Individual teams need to know, remember, and embrace this vision.

The act of turning up and going into the office every day was an immediate, natural re-alignment to the larger company, the purpose and the long-term strategy of the organization. The employee would be back in the fold without even thinking about it.

Times have changed, people are now isolated from the bigger picture of what they are doing and where they work.

Work no longer necessarily has a physical location in the world. It now belongs in the non-tangible virtual space with a more significant imprint on google than the pavement.

If you don't keep the larger and long-term mission statements of your company at the forefront, it will be all too easy to disconnect from them completely.

It is crucial to keep people involved in what they are doing outside of their role. They need to know that they are part of a wider company and not just secluded to a department with their to-do list and targets to reach; what they do has an impact on the company as a whole.

The larger the organization, the more complicated this becomes.

This takes work. It is a continual effort on your part to ensure everyone is staying connected with why they work at your company - and what the point of them (virtually) turning up every day is.

I have found rhythm to be the most successful way of achieving this. By this I mean you need to regularly remind people of the bigger goals of the company.

If it becomes boring, dry and repetitive people will zone out. You have to be inventive and work out methods to keep your company ethos resonating with the rest of the team.

Validation and Celebration

Success breeds more positive success.

This builds momentum in a team, and you can do a lot to enable and encourage this as the leader.

PRINCIPLE 6:
Highlight, promote and even manufacture positivity

People want to work on a winning team and contribute to that success.

We have lost the little celebrations and congratulations on a job well done that happens in the office. It's all too easy to focus on the troubles, especially when it seems like the whole world is struggling.

In your meetings, you need to find out what people have accomplished in the week and celebrate it.

Break big projects down into small milestones, track them in your weekly meetings, and celebrate checking each one off. It's a little hit of collective dopamine, and you're creating a culture of achieving and success.

Drawing attention to success reinforces accomplishment in your team. You can remind them that it's possible to achieve even in the hard times. After all, a win's a win, and a job well done deserves to be recognised.

Progress is a great motivator, and you need to find projects for people to rally around.

You can track your progress as a team with the development of a project. At weekly meetings, you can highlight the developments made through the use of graphs, filling in blocks as a visual indicator of progress.

This is a small thing that can go a long way to building overall team positivity and establishing a sense of achievement.

People like to be recognised in different ways. What makes one person cringe will make another glow with pride.

An introvert may be embarrassed and shy about receiving praise in front of a group. These individuals appreciate a message or an email to show that you recognised their work instead. Others (extroverts I'm looking at you) really thrive when they are recognised in front of a group.

Here's some tips for giving praise;

» **Slow down** and check they are in the right frame of mind to receive it, that they are listening and present.

» **Get serious**, look them in the eye and speak authentically.

» **Be specific** - talk about exactly what they did and when they did it, highlight any obstacles they had to navigate, sacrifices they made, and benefits brought on by it. Highlight the overall positive effect.

Of course, you need to be praising them for something worthwhile. Don't make things up or give praise for something relatively trivial.

Try not to get caught up in their response, many people are shy. Even if they brush off the praise, ("it was no big deal" or "it was a team effort") they still heard it, and it's a powerful way of letting someone know that they were seen and that they matter.

Running Successful Online Meetings

At the moment, it seems like the day can turn into one online meeting after another. The hours gained in the lack of commute have been given over to zoom calls.

Companies are meeting virtually more than ever, it's time to learn some best practices to thrive online.

If your meetings are dull and uninspired people will tune out, no one will engage, and your culture will suffer.

In this next section, you'll learn a whole set of tools, tactics, and techniques to run fast-moving, energetic, productive meetings.

Set the Rules

Be crystal clear about what your expectations and objectives are for meetings.

I suggest you create a "meeting charter" which lays out the exact rules that people are expected to follow. The more specific you can be in your expectations, the better it is for everyone.

It's a big help for new members of staff who will be able to look to it for a clear understanding of what's expected of them too.

Here are some things to consider when creating your own meeting charter:

> » Is video required? If so when?

> » Are people required to turn up on time?

> » Are people able to take other calls or answer emails during a meeting?

» Are people allowed to put themselves on mute?

You can also create guidelines for making sure that there's a clear objective to the meeting such as:

» Who should/should not be invited to the meeting

» Recording/transcribing/recapping the meeting

» How long meetings should be

» Who takes what role in the meeting (taking notes, reviewing to-do's, posting recordings, scheduling follow-ups, etc.)

Review the objectives at the beginning of the meeting. This initial check-in will make sure everyone is still in line with the agenda before you progress.

Send the meeting objectives along with any required reading/research at least 24 hours beforehand. This enables you to get right to the point when the meeting starts.

Enforcing these rules is part of the "art" of leadership. The more you let them slip, the more disorganised and ineffectual your meetings will become.

PRINCIPLE 7:
Run tight meetings. Period.

Once people see that you're serious about holding everyone accountable, they will be much more likely to follow the rules.

Your team will be grateful that you are respecting their time by being as efficient and focused as possible.

Just imagine if you could cut your meeting times down by half and still get the job done, all while people respect you *more* as their leader.

Train in the Basics

Being in an online meeting may seem an ordinary practise for some, but it's a totally new experience for others.

A few minutes of basic training can make all the difference to the quality of your calls. You need to teach people how to position themselves for the camera and how to use a microphone.

It may seem obvious... but lighting is everything. Tell your team to make sure that they are adequately lit, so they are not sitting in shadow or darkness. If you, or a team member, are working somewhere that has limited lighting, you can buy ring lighting from Amazon that can lift your lighting game.

The position of your face in the frame is important too. If you're too close you'll be projecting an unflattering angle of full face. (Think accidental selfie-style when your phone is accidentally set to the front camera - no one likes that double chin.)

If you're too far away from the camera, you'll be tiny on the screen. This makes it difficult for other people to connect to you - your body language and facial expressions will be too hard to read. Remember, we're going for as much eye contact as possible. Ideally, you will be in the centre of the frame, like a passport photo.

Sound quality can make or break a meeting. Think about when you're listening to music or a podcast. How irritating is it when it's flickering in and out, and you only catch bits and pieces? Or you've got that reverb sound, so things are echoing or jittering? Doesn't it make you want to throw your phone/laptop/ipad out the window?

It's the same with online meetings. At the very least consider investing in a decent microphone which doesn't make that irritating echo noise. No one wants to hear their own voice being thrown back at them.

Have your team watch and listen to themselves in an actual meeting, then they can see how they are presenting to the group.

Here's a website that makes it amazingly easy to test your own setup https://webcammictest.com/

Technology Support

In times like this, you should give your team outstanding technical support and training. It's a total morale destroyer when you're trying to get your job done, and the technology is keeping you from working. An employee with a good set-up is a happy and productive employee.

Don't cut corners and save money on inadequate equipment and poor personal IT support. You will also have to figure out guidelines on who pays for broadband and equipment upgrades etc.

If you do have that support in place, make sure people are aware of it and know how to take advantage of that.

Shorten your Meetings

A previous boss of mine once told me that nobody ever makes money in internal meetings.

Internal meetings can be very valuable. However, they are an expensive use of time. With this in mind, I do everything I can to make sure they run smoothly and effectively.

My team appreciates that and takes my meetings seriously. They show up prepared, and on time, they are present the whole way through, and we accomplish our meeting goals every time.

I'm going to set you a challenge right now.

Go to your calendar and look at the meetings you have scheduled in the next three days. Ask yourself what would happen if you cut the time for each of them in half?

According to Parkinson's law, "a meeting expands to fill the time it's scheduled for". Set aside an hour, you will fill that hour. Take the same content but give yourself 30 minutes, you will achieve delivering that same content in a smaller time frame.

My default meeting time is 25 minutes. There are no rules to say you can't schedule an even shorter (15 or 10 minutes) meeting. You would be surprised how easy it is to get to the point when you have to. Cut out the waffle and be specific, it frees up extra time in the day for everyone.

There are caveats with this of course. Creativity can take time, and you also want to make sure people are heard.

It can be tempting to use meetings for some networking time as it's something that we're missing in the remote working world. However, I would suggest that this should be handled separately outside of meeting times.

Going back to your upcoming meetings, this time ask yourself if everyone invited really needs to be there.

Having someone sit through a long meeting that they aren't needed for is a big waste of time - not to mention demoralizing and expensive (after all, the more people at a meeting, the more it's going to cost).

If you are recording or transcribing meetings, they can be sent round later, or you can catch someone up later with the cliff notes. If you have an extended group meeting where a person is only needed for one topic, begin there so that person can leave after their section has been discussed.

With this efficient and formal approach to meetings, you need to make sure that there are social outlets and opportunities for people to connect on a more informal level.

Starting on Time

A pet peeve of mine is when a meeting starts late.

Timekeeping in a virtual environment is slightly more complicated because it can take a few minutes for technology to connect.

Tell your team that meetings are going to start exactly on time and ask them to enter the meeting room 2 or 3 minutes early with this in mind.

The best way to get this started, team or company-wide, is to diligently follow this rule yourself. Always start your meetings early, enter meetings that other people are hosting early, and let the team know that you expect this from them.

It might take a few gos for people to adapt, and you might find a few late joiners to begin with. Stick with it, people will follow your example.

Getting Everyone Involved

It's up to you to make sure everyone is included in every meeting.

When leading a meeting that will be over 20 minutes, with three or more people, start by involving everyone right away. You could have everyone give a "one-word" opener. This is where each person would state how they are feeling at that moment in one word only.

Another tactic is to have people share a highlight and a lowlight from the last week. This allows your team to have a brag, celebrate the victories and even air some frustrations. It can be a subtle way to stay on the pulse of what's going on for people.

In senior leadership meetings, I have asked each person, myself included, to rate themselves from 1 to 10 professionally and personally. This exercise allows me to gain an accurate gauge of where people are at. It has often opened up critical discussions on where and when people need support. This technique is only useful in a small, well-established group with a high level of trust.

Psychologically, these techniques can open up the space and encourage people to speak up and stay engaged throughout the meeting.

Extroverts & Introverts in Meetings

You will rarely have a meeting of purely introverted or purely extrovert personality types, your average meeting will be a mix.

Your challenge will be to ensure that the extroverts on the call don't dominate the meeting. These individuals will be fit to burst if they have been working home alone all day with no one to talk to. They will expend all this pent up social energy talking through the whole meeting.

You need to recognise, manage and even coach their behaviour, in and out of the meeting.

During the meeting, you can stop them in their tracks with a gentle reminder that "we need to hear from everyone" or "I'm getting confused, what's the main point that you're making?" Outside the meeting, and one-to-one, you can reflect back on their behaviour and challenge them to work on their brevity and focus on what they intend to share.

Make this about their future professional development; if they want to progress, they will need these skills in higher-level meetings. Senior leaders appreciate people who can directly get to the point.

Your challenge with introverts is the opposite, make sure you are giving these individuals a chance and the platform to have their input.

These quieter types are often listening intently to everything happening, even though they may not have been so active in the discussion. As a result, they are more likely to see the bigger picture, or have noticed some vital content while reflecting on what everyone else is saying.

I've been in many a meeting where everybody has been gabbing away, then the leader asks one of the quieter people for their opinion. This person gathers their thoughts and then proceeds to deliver an essential piece of insight that changes the paradigm of the discussion.

An introvert will typically prefer a little time to get themselves together rather than speaking off the cuff. Give these people the heads up that you're about to ask for their input. For example, you could say "Barb, we're going to hear from you in a second, right after Mary gives us her update".

Give an introvert time to speak, there may be some pauses in the delivery. Don't let anyone else talk over them - this should already be a rule, no matter the personality type. If someone interrupts, politely stop them and allow the person with the floor to finish. You only have to be firm with this a few times, people catch on quickly and respect you for stepping in and setting the boundaries.

One final tactic that I use when getting input on an issue is to go around the room and give everyone one minute to speak their mind.

Everyone will get the opportunity to have the floor, and they know to finish their thought within 60 seconds.

If you're looking for more ideas, come join us in the group by going to tiny.cc/leadersgroup and joining, we would love to hear what's working for you too.

Culture & Accountability

Holding people accountable for their actions and behaviours is a vital, yet complicated, component to successful leadership.

Accountability becomes even more challenging when your team is working remotely.

Here we'll talk about ways to hold people accountable from a positive, empowering place, in a way that it becomes natural and part of the culture.

When it's done right, people and teams hold themselves accountable.

PRINCIPLE 8:
Empowered accountability leads
to a strong culture.

There is a big difference between micromanaging, supporting people, correcting them, and delegating.

Micromanagement is the hallmark of a poor leader.

This type of leader will take too much control, dictating to their people how they should do every little piece of their jobs, and focusing on the process instead of the result. It displays a lack of trust in your team and can be highly frustrating for anyone working for you.

You need to give your team members the tools and the freedom to achieve in their roles.

This may seem harder in the remote way of working, but it's even more important to implement now people aren't in the office.

PRINCIPLE 9:
Focus on results and outcomes, not on time or process

Many leaders have commented on how they are secretly worried that some people aren't working the hours they are supposed to, or the hours that they claim to be.

I've even seen software packages intended for remote workers that record and track everything they do. This way, the managers are sure they are putting in a full day's work.

This hasn't been my experience with the successful teams I've been involved with.

Don't focus on how much time people are putting in, or even how they get things done. Instead, get clear on what the individual's output and results should be and put the full focus on that. It shows trust in your team and gives them the freedom to be creative and find the best way to do their jobs.

If you revert to micromanaging and counting hours, they will put in the time and then clock off when that allotted time is up. If you empower them to find the best way to reach their goals themselves, they will probably spend extra time figuring out how to do their part for the team.

Make sure you are still there for support and schedule regular check-ins - this is not micromanaging.

When you assign a task to somebody, make the next milestone clear - in structure, intent and when the next check-in is. People will get much more job satisfaction because you are trusting them and they know you believe them to be capable.

Give your team the tools to succeed, don't take control of the journey.

CASE STUDY

I'm currently coaching a manager who gave a task to one of his teammates.

He has yet to hear back from her. He has no idea of what's going on with the task. Understandably, the lack of communication is making him anxious and more than a little bit frustrated.

I asked for the specific details on the task. He had given a broad brief with no detailed action plans or time frame in place. There was little direction on how the team member should complete the task, it left her up to her own devices.

I worked with him to develop a better plan of action for the next time he needed to direct or delegate a task to avoid this stress and confusion moving forward.

Always schedule a date in the calendar with what the deliverables are expected to be at that point. This needs to be a time frame that allows for a significant amount of the task to be done, but not so much time that things can slide or go in the wrong direction.

In this case, the manager had delegated the task of updating the firms' internal processes to his accounts manager. This was a complicated task, he needed to take the time to make sure that she understood the whole job and then work with her to come up with a gameplan. This enabled him to guide his teammate but also allowed her to take the initiative of designing her own framework.

He was able to share his wisdom, experience, and expectations in a way that gave her the freedom to incorporate her ideas and learn from him at the same time. By the end of the process, they had a mutually agreed-upon plan of action.

Moving forward, I suggested he schedule a catch up within a week or two, even if it was for only 5 or 10 minutes. By that time, he would expect his team member to have one of the processes updated. They could review her output together, and he would be able to make suggestions or modifications at that early stage.

This would be her first time processing in this way - mistakes are bound to be made. It would be prudent to pick this up sooner, rather than later, so she can make amends and learn from it, instead of making the same mistake on all the processes.

> The manager stepped back and then stepped back in at a predetermined point. He did not look over her shoulder and dictate her every move. Due to this action, he was able to focus on the results and ensure that his teammate delivered a quality output.

Trust is an essential factor when dealing with a remote workforce.

You have no way of seeing what your team members are doing, or how they are, by getting up and taking a stroll around the office. You have to trust that they are going to get things done without you looking over their shoulder.

This doesn't mean you don't review or quality control their work, but it does mean that you have to let go of that desire to know what they're doing all the time.

It's time to shift the focus from time at the desk to output and results.

Make sure people are clear on what the expectations are from them in their role, and give them the freedom to explore those expectations. Have agreed times when people in your team are available to collaborate and answer questions.

Teams that are heavily involved in programming and coding can allocate a 2-4 hour window when they can be reached for calls and meetings. Leave the rest of the day clear so they can crack on with their technical workload. This way, people can experience their own accountability and responsibility within the framework of check-in and reviews.

A team-wide platform can be a great way of encouraging accountability in your team members.

If you are assigning people specific tasks in your weekly meetings, review what each task is at the end of the session, whose responsibility it is and the due date.

When the next meeting rolls around, the first action point is to assess the tasks set last week and the progress made with each task. It's really embarrassing to stand up (virtually or not) and admit that you haven't completed something in such a public platform.

If this happens multiple weeks in a row, then there's obviously an issue, and you can deal with it directly. It rarely gets to that point, nobody wants to let the team down. By asking people to state their success or failure at completing the task, it becomes particularly personal.

Procrastination can create a vicious cycle of anxiety. If a team member is procrastinating on a project they are falling behind on, it leads to stress and anxiety. This stress fosters further procrastination, increasing anxiety levels. You can wind up in a bit of a mental-health hole.

To limit the temptation to procrastinate, make projects and progress visible so people can see how well they are accomplishing their goals. This transparency supports your team by keeping them on task and not having people fall behind.

With the increased visibility of project progress and tracking the achievements made throughout the week, there is more incentive for the team to get things done. This will lead to gains in confidence and a surge of positive energy, creating a more engaged workforce with less chance of burn out.

This is a solid foundation for a happier, healthier and more productive team.

It doesn't have to be about changing one huge thing within your company, implementing lots of little things to encourage this positive mindset and accepting accountability can have a powerful impact.

It takes some discipline to put the changes in place, but once there, they will gain momentum and become a habit in no time at all.

Cross Collaboration

Natural cross-collaboration between teams has been lost through remote working.

The impromptu conversations at the coffee station or water cooler, or even the ability to pop out for lunch together, are no longer a part of the day.

These spontaneous events were an integral part of feeling connected to the company as a whole. An informal chat could wind up with someone in production forming a great working relationship with someone in IT. These are the moments when work friends are made, and a network is built.

Not only is that a positive for an individual's career, but it creates a break - it can lift someone's mood and makes the working day better.

Unfortunately, there is no way to bring these scenarios back informally. You have to be intentional about organizing them instead.

Create opportunities for people to have a coffee, a meal, or a drink etc. with other members of the organization. You could instigate a "coffee and cake" break in the office calendar on zoom a few times a week. This might just be a short 10-15minutes online slot at 11am where people could join the meeting if they wanted to, and have a brief chat over a coffee and a biscuit.

It's easy to get locked down and locked into your own screen. Working away on your own, you forget that there are other people in other departments working towards the same overall purpose as you.

As a bonus, these scheduled socials are an excellent way for new employees to meet people in different departments and really start to feel connected to the broader company.

Informal get-togethers contribute to peer-to-peer engagement and help to build a sense of community.

Onboarding

Onboarding is a tricky scenario that most companies find challenging even at the best of times. This has been made even more complicated with the shift to remote working.

Remote, office and hybrid working are all in occurrence right now - with many companies making the move to fully remote working for the foreseeable future. As a result, you have to put a major effort into onboarding a new employee.

It's difficult to make connections with people you do know through a webcam, let alone building new relationships or feeling part of a team of people that you've never met in the flesh.

CASE STUDY

One CEO and co-founder that I spoke to used the first lockdown to upgrade his teams. He needed highly technical people for the role, and these are hard to find in his industry. For each new employee, he assigned a buddy, (a peer at the same level) and a mentor (a colleague who was either higher up or more experienced).

The buddy's responsibility was to check in with the new employee from time-to-time to see how they were getting on. The mentor relationship was more formal in nature.

In addition to this system, the CEO himself ensured that he spent time chatting with the new hire.

After getting to know them a little better, he asked them if there was anything that they wanted to ask him, in a less formal setting, that might have been uncomfortable during the interview process.

This allowed the CEO to show openness and approachability while also enabling them to connect on a deeper level.

Before the stricter lockdown came into full swing, the CEO organised a socially distanced Happy Hour in a local park to give people the opportunity to meet face-to-face. Partners and families were invited, and the event was a big hit.

This is a perfect example of a company being inventive and creative to bring people together and build team spirit despite the restrictions in place.

There's so much I can share with you about getting intentional about your cultures and your values, but I'll save that for another book. If this is something you are really keen to know more about, you can always reach out to me directly at RMichaelAnderson.com/contact/

Buddy system

Some companies have found a simple "buddy system" works well. This is particularly effective if you have new people joining the company. This system can also encourage new relationships with long-standing members of staff that may not interact with different areas of the company.

You can match people up and have them catch up with each other every day - a virtual water cooler or a cup of coffee moment. Consider a switch up or a rotation every few weeks or months for variety.

Be mindful of your pairings - an extreme introvert and an extreme extrovert are likely to antagonise each other, or just fail to have anything in common which may just create extra stress.

Introverts checking in with introverts is a great pairing, as is extroverts checking in with extroverts - they will communicate and respond in a similar way.

If you do implement this, ensure you are still checking in with one-to-ones and group sessions. This does not replace that contact you have on a personal level with your team.

PART 4

The Next Normal

Your Go-Forward Strategy

It's time to talk about where to go from here.

This section gives a high-level overview of what a go-forward strategy looks like from a corporate, leadership, and workforce standpoint. I will be discussing the essential components that you need to understand to help your team moving forward.

Assumptions and Predictions

2020 sent shock waves around the world. No one could have predicted just how dramatically we would all be affected by the virus.

However, we now have no excuse to be blindsided by something like this again. We should be fully pandemic prepared and ready for all eventualities.

The vaccine is not a magical solution to all that's happened. It certainly won't be a quick fix - there's a lot of people in the world to vaccinate, and it will be a while before it gets anywhere close to being safe again.

Experts are estimating that a return to any sense of normalcy - where we can travel freely, end social distancing, and throw away our masks - won't be until summer 2021 in a best-case scenario.

That doesn't even take into account when consumer spending and government assistance programs will revert to normal. It could be a long time for the economy to recover; post vaccine and post-pandemic does not mean the world will be as though 2020 never happened.

Hopefully, the vaccine will be enough to change things, and it will eradicate or minimize the effects of the virus, allowing us to rebuild and thrive. However, there's also a very good chance that this virus may mutate, there may be a new virus or another major event that disrupts you and your business.

As leaders, we need to rebuild our teams, our companies, and our mindset to be ready for whatever normal is next, and the normal after that.

After all, that's what your competitors are doing.

A Post-Downturn Meta-Analysis

In the summer of 2020, I teamed up with Dr. Nick Quinn at the University of Glasgow Adam Smith Business School to look at what the "winners" of previous downturns did to set them apart.

We gathered over 15 pieces of research from institutions like McKinsey, Bain Capital and Harvard. We wanted to help business leaders learn what they needed to do to bounce back strong as things get better..

.

Your True Competitive Advantage

A supply chain, distribution system, and market share used to be competitive advantages, but they are not sustainable and can crumble in the face of a lockdown. The systems built over decades were destroyed in the weeks, or a few months, of enforced closures.

Outside of assets and intellectual property (which never goes out of style!) we've learned something new:

PRINCIPLE 10:
Your culture, agility, and people are your
long-term competitive advantages.

We were already in a fast-changing world. After being under the microscope for nearly a year, we know that being rigid and inflexible is beneficial to no-one. Change and modifications don't just happen here and there. Being adaptable is something that needs to be built into the fabric of your company.

With change comes opportunity. Think back over 2020, what do you wish you did sooner? What do you wish you took advantage of - even though your team wasn't ready to execute it fast enough?

Each company - and each team - has an "Identity". What is the identity of your team? How would the team members characterize it? How would your peers, or others outside of your team, describe it?

You need to create a culture that normalizes change. This will build resilience in everyone's mindset. This is easier said than done. However, when you have a strong team, who believes in your leadership because they know you support them as people, they will find a way to win.

Unwavering Pragmatic Optimism

The nuts and bolts strategy goes with an overarching mindset that needs to come from you and all the leaders.

PRINCIPLE 11:
Unwavering pragmatic optimism fuels
the rest of the strategy.

As I have mentioned before, people need to believe in you. They need to know that their leaders have faith in where they are going.

You need more than just optimism, you need this optimism to be unshakeable. You can't fake it, and you can't show any cracks. People will see straight through that and give up hope.

Your optimism has to be practical. No one will believe unrealistic expectations. If you lay out an unreachable goal that you don't achieve, you'll lose credibility for the next time.

When you do embrace this unwavering pragmatic optimism, you bring a refreshed energy to everything. Remember all that you learned in the previous section about communication and vulnerability - it all goes together, and here's where you can apply it.

Have a Clear Pivot Point

Many companies haven't yet gathered themselves enough to fully formulate a new strategy to communicate to the organization.

Now that we're past the sprint and into the marathon, the senior leadership team needs to design a holistic strategy for the entire organization.

When you have a concise, well thought out strategy, you can effectively communicate the direction of the entire company. You will be able to break it down and establish how that plan will affect each person.

By only giving small amounts of strategic information to team members left, right and centre, you come across as disjointed and reactionary. You need to get all the pieces in place before the point of delivery. People will listen, understand, and get on board with the whole plan, and you'll come across as more strategic and thoughtful.

Parallel Processes

Take the time to figure out a proper strategy, but don't wait to give your team what they need. Empathy, authentic communication, one-to-one conversations, social connecting, time off, well-being training, and more should be implemented right away.

When I work with clients, we usually address the issues of team health and new leadership skills immediately. The strategy is in the background while we really focus on the people.

When we interact with teams and management, we get a much greater sense of what's truly going on in the departments. This helps to create a much more grounded and effective strategy.

Company Strategy

I've broken down strategy into two parts; company (or organizational) strategy, and workforce strategy.

The workforce strategy is what you need to address when moving to a hybrid or fully virtual workforce.

Operational Resilience

Your company needs to be able to adapt and make decisions quickly. It's been found that small, agile teams who are empowered to make decisions far outperform the traditional, top-down, bureaucratic teams of the past.

You can't just take a team, tell them they are empowered and have them make decisions. This is a trust, culture, and structural issue. It comes from the type of relationship that is formed over time and from supportive company culture.

The team needs to be structured correctly. What type of decisions can people make and what can they not? What decision-making process should they go through? How will they be compensated, supported, and evaluated?

Technology, Technology, Technology

Technology can be 'The Great Enabler'. However, as a former programmer and tech geek myself, I see many companies not understanding or embracing it properly.

Technology is not a tool, it's your new platform of business - especially when you move to decentralization, e-commerce, and virtual working. Every level of management needs to understand and support it. You need a proper technology strategy, strong tech leadership, and to understand the business impacts of tech in your business.

If people have issues when they are working at home, and you are not able to make decisions supported by data, you have a problem.

If you don't have real-time (or close to real-time) profitability by product, product line, geography, customer, customer type, and every other dimension, it's time to make a change.

The good thing is that it's easier than ever to solve these issues.

Simplify and Focus

It's time to figure out exactly where you want to go. Strip it all back and let go of anything else that's not involved with your core business aim.

We need healthy, resilient, and engaged teams. Adapting to change takes a lot of energy, this is not something we have to spare. Every ounce of power should be invested in value-added activities we know will produce a short to medium term ROI.

Let go of your "pet projects", divest any business unit, product, or line of business that's a distraction to your primary business. Get clear on what your core business is going forward.

Your finite resources, cash and people's energy, need to be laser-focused on revenue and profitability, anything you can sell-off to stockpile more cash or will support you over the longer term.

Be careful of what you gamble on.

CEO's may want to acquire companies, and there are many bargains to be had out there right now. If the integration is complex, and there's no clear payback in the next 12 months, it may be more of a cash drain and distraction than you can manage right now.

There's a surprising amount of corporate bankruptcies as a post-downturn rebound happens because firms get overconfident and overextend themselves.

Don't be one of those casualties.

Necessary Investments

Dr. Quinn and I found that there are a few vital areas where companies cannot afford to reduce or stop investing in. These are sales, marketing, people, research & development, and technology.

In previous downturns, companies that held back on sales and marketing found that they lost momentum, and some could never get it back. In many cases, they had to resort to discounting to keep revenue up. This ate into profitability and overall cash flow.

Some organizations actually use downturns to gain market share as advertising and marketing may be less expensive. Samsung did this in the great recession. In 2009 they heavily marketed the Galaxy line of phones and tablets. In addition to becoming a major player in the market, this moved their brand ranking from 21 to 6 globally.

One consistent message I'm hearing is how difficult it is to create new relationships and prospect new leads, especially in B2B. (If I get one more templated LinkedIn request from someone trying to sell me something I may just punch my computer.)

People need continued investment, and Research & Development is essential. When there is marketplace change, your products and services need to adapt as well.

Workforce Strategy

Creating a high-performing hybrid or entirely virtual team is possible when taking a strategic approach.

Something I've learned in my many years of leadership is that almost everyone wants to be a productive member of a team. It's up to us to create the conditions to make that happen.

PRINCIPLE 12:
Everyone wants to be a great team member,
it's your job to let them.

Since you're used to an office-based environment, there are subtle and major shifts and changes that need to be addressed.

Our calculations show that while it will be a next cost savings, and you will probably save considerably on rent and facilities, more spend will go to technology and employee connection.

Some of the savings made needs to be re-allocated to this new way of working.

Safety is your Priority

For people coming back to an office or a work event - even for a single meeting - an active virus out there can be very stressful.

Remember that some people are high-risk or have high-risk households. Don't make assumptions and don't force people into potentially risky conditions. Err on the side of caution.

There's a whole lot of questions that need to be answered now, including;

» What happens if someone tests positive for COVID who's been at the office?

» What happens if someone tests positive for COVID who's been working at home?

» What if someone passes away from COVID?

» What happens if an employee has to care for a relative with COVID?

» What are the local regulatory & legal issues about workplace safety?

» What if someone refuses to work?

» How can you avoid that happening in the first place by extra caution and communications?

There are also a lot of workplace safety issues concerning PPE, re-entry, monitoring, cleaning, food safety, and more.

Guiding Principles

The mission, values, and purpose of the organization are your guiding principles.

You may have an entirely different business model, way of working and focus post-pandemic. Moving forward for you as a company is a "re-introduction" of your business to your employees.

It's the prime time to review, update, and recommit to your guiding principles. This will help define your new culture and support everyone, as well as your goals and initiatives going forward.

Human Resources Redefined

Over the past few decades, we've realized that humans aren't just resources. Our HR departments have shifted into supporting and helping people grow.

In this next step, we have to make sure that HR is going to be there to keep everyone on top of their (remote) game. However, HR is the enabler rather than the cost centre - make sure that senior leadership stays involved.

The structure of HR is going to have to adapt too. I've talked to leaders who went from recruiting locally - so the team can come into the office - to recruiting globally. Your recruiting, onboarding and employee termination should all be reconsidered.

A new way of working comes with a new skills profile and a new skill gap analysis for everyone, including higher level and leadership.

A work-at-home policy must be well thought out and introduced company-wide. There's a lot of questions that need to be answered with regards to that. What time(s) do you expect people to be available for meetings? Who pays for internet connectivity? How does a hardware issue get fixed?

As a former CEO, I can tell you these types of questions aren't my favorite to handle. However, they are crucial to supporting and being of service to your team. These problems aren't going to magically disappear, you need to deal with them.

Spend the extra time to make sure the policy is clear and comprehensive. It needs to be fair, and it needs to be appropriately communicated to existing and new employees. You could have employee representatives help formulate these strategies.

Make sure your Employee Assistance Program (EAP) is up to date for your new way of working and that everyone knows how to access it. If you're not aware, an EAP offers confidential counselling services to support well-being in the workplace and in the personal lives for your staff. Some programs even extend to immediate family members.

High-Performance Teams

It takes more than ensuring the good mental and physical health of your people to form a long-term high performing team. To develop real "A" players for your organization, you need to focus on developing the structure, support and incentives.

An incentive can come from compensation, but this is less expenditure than you might think. However, a much more sustainable motivation comes from being a key part of a winning team.

Daniel Pink talks about how people are motivated in his book Drive: The Surprising Truth About What Motivates Us. Pink discusses how people are motivated by purpose, autonomy, and mastery.

It is crucial to have a purpose for your organization and even an individual one for your team. People crave the freedom to make a difference on their own (autonomy), and the ability to do their job to the best of their ability (mastery.) As a leader, you can enable these pillars. Focus on objectives instead of counting the hours of your team, and provide training and coaching so they can solve problems themselves.

With a new company strategy in place, you will want to revisit the compensation structure, incentives, and employee review process to make sure everything is in alignment.

You'll also want to review your meeting rhythms and come up with new KPI's / OKR's / metrics to make sure you are managing and leading proactively.

Leadership Development

Leaders need support too.

This is a new world, make sure your leaders are getting the help, tools and skills they need to manage in this new climate.

From the survey conducted for this book, we can see that senior managers are the group struggling the most with mental health issues.

This is hardly surprising.

Managers are bearing so much of the responsibility for managing and leading this change. Many leaders I talked to are so focused on supporting their people that they forget about themselves.

Closing Thoughts

Change isn't always easy, it's rarely fun, but it is almost always necessary.

In my experience, if we, as leaders, look at change as a challenge to grow and improve, everyone wins in the end.

Take a minute. Reflect on how many people you affect with your decisions. This includes your staff, peers, customers, investors and even family and friends.

Now take another minute, close your eyes and visualize yourself. See yourself as that transformational leader that brings about positive change for everyone.

If you don't step up, who will?

Asking for help in these times is not failing. Having the humility to recognize you need a hand can help you survive and thrive.

If you want to reach out to me personally to see how my team and I can help your situation, do so by going here: RMichaelAnderson.com/contact

If you would like additional resources, training, and to be part of an incredible community of other forward-thinking leaders, join the companion group by going to this link: tiny.cc/leadersgroup

Hopefully, I've achieved my purpose in writing this book, and it's given you some tools and strategies to make your life, and the people you affect, just that much better.

Lead On,

Michael

APPENDIX I

The Healthy Leader

A guide to making sure you're fit on the inside and out

This bonus appendix is a quick guide to cover the physical, mental, and emotional health aspects you should be taking care of. You need to be at the top of the game during this time.

You may know a lot of what's covered, and even if you do, use this as a reminder to get those positive habits back into your routine.

In each section are hacks and quick-tips to give you the most benefit as quickly and simply as possible.

Your Energy Tank

Your energy tank is a metaphor for the finite amount of energy available to you every day.

Think of it as your own personal fuel tank that you refill every night when you go to sleep. The amount of fuel you start with, and what you expend during the day is very much in your control.

If you exercise the day before, get a full night's sleep, and start the morning with a nutritious breakfast, you're starting out with a whole lot of fuel in your tank. If you got drunk the night before following a stressful and inactive day, slept a few restless hours and skipped breakfast, your fuel tank is going to be heavily depleted.

Eating healthy meals during the day, taking regular breaks and incorporating a walk outside will keep that fuel tank stoked. You're going to make better decisions, interact with your team more effectively and have a much higher quality of life.

How much of these simple lifestyle habits are you integrating into your life?

Stress punches holes in our fuel tanks. Some are big and obvious while others are tiny and insidious - the longer they are there, the more damage that is done.

Significant stress might be a personal trauma like a death, restructuring or redundancy at work, or an upcoming exam. Small stress could be feeling unworthy or unconfident in a job, personal insecurities or even dreading your daily office zoom call. As a one-off, these small stressors wouldn't be so much of an issue, but day in and day out they grow in magnitude and impact on your overall stress load.

COVID-19, the election, Brexit, terrorist attacks and natural disasters are all events that we bear witness to as a collective, this is stress experienced by everyone that is continuous in the background of our lives.

We are constantly bombarded with imagery and information. Social media has enabled us to be more aware of collective stress than ever before. We are repeatedly hit with the data of micro and macro traumas. This adds to our individual stress load and takes a toll on the body.

Think about your body as a computer. If you overload the system with multiple programs, it's going to run slow. If you have a virus active in the background, nothing is going to function effectively. Every virus, every program is a stress on the system. You have to find that virus and close down some of the programs to run at optimum speed and efficiency.

It's essential to look, really look, and reflect on the amount of stress that may be impacting your life and affecting your overall health and wellbeing.

Your Physical Fuel

Let's start with diet and what you're fueling your body with.

If you put petrol in a diesel car, that car is never going to run right. It's the same with the body.

And before we go too much further, here is a list of things that are NOT healthy:

» Yogurt - this is nothing but fat and sugar...more like a dessert than breakfast. If you are going to eat yogurt, choose a natural unsweetened yogurt with live cultures.

» Boxed Cereal - this is just a bunch of processed chemicals masked with sugar.

» Breakfast Sandwich (i.e. bacon/eggs on bread/toast) - the combo of a simple carb with protein means it may fill you up but won't sustain energy.

» Croissant/Pastries/Pancakes/Waffles/French Toast - lots of sugar and fatty ingredients will lead to a short lived energy boost followed by the dreaded mid-morning crash.

» Commercial smoothies or fruit juice - these are just packed with sugar. Homemade smoothies using mainly vegetables with some fruit and added protein powder is a much more sustainable fuel source. Avoid fatty milk and added sweeteners.

» Sugar is sugar. While honey and maple syrup are more agreeable forms - your body still recognises and uses them as sugar.

If you crash in the mind-morning, afternoon or lack energy all day, then here are some quick hacks that have helped to keep me going.

I'm going to give you two effortless recipes to follow. These are nutritious, easy, and a good tasting breakfast and lunch every day.

Overnight Oats

Ingredients
» Oat flakes - not the instant packaged kind
» Milk - regular cows milk or any alternative milk
» Blueberries/raisins/cinnamon (optional)
» A little honey or Maple syrup (optional)

Before you go to bed:
» take out a bowl and fill it halfway with oat flakes.
» Cover the oat flakes with milk.
» Pop it in the fridge overnight.

Voila! When you wake up, you have a straightforward, quick breakfast. You can put blueberries, raisins, cinnamon, even a little bit of honey or Maple syrup on it to give it some flavor.

Don't make it too sweet - it's not supposed to be a dessert.

Line the stomach before reaching for that first cup of coffee. Coffee on an empty stomach can cause long term issues.

If you don't have time for breakfast first thing, you can substitute the bowl for a Tupperware so you can take it with you and eat later.

Do you skip breakfast? Do you find yourself lagging, irritable or fatigued through the morning? Try a small bowl or even a mug of this in the morning to start your day. See if you feel any different.

Lasting Lunch

Ingredients
» Leaves - any green you like - lettuce, rocket, spinach, kale
» Fresh vegetables - peppers/tomatoes/radish/beetroot/avocado
» Protein of choice - Hummus, tuna fish, chicken, walnuts
» Extra Virgin Olive Oil - or any non-dairy dressing

The best and easiest thing to do is to make a salad with fresh vegetables and dressing along with some tuna fish or hummus as a protein.

You can make this the night before as well. If you've cooked or roasted vegetables with dinner, save some to add to your salad the next day. Just make sure to use a non-dairy dressing - something like blue cheese or ranch has more calories than a full plate of food and will slow you down later as well.

If you want something carby in there consider sweet potato or a piece of rye bread. Avoid things like croutons as they add no nutritional value and are likely to cause a blood sugar spike. Long, slow-released energy is what we're going for here.

The more diverse you can make your food, the better - this can be achieved by rotating the vegetables and protein source within the salad.

Simple Snack
Ingredients
» Banana or apple

» Unsalted raw nuts or unsweetened nut butter

» Sliced apple or banana with some nut butter or raw nuts is a great in-between meal healthy snack.

If you have trouble digesting nuts - try soaking them in water overnight.

The sugar of the fruit combined with the protein and fats in the nuts taste delicious and will keep you full without the sugar spike and crash.

The way we eat it is as important as what we eat. Where possible, try to eat away from your desk and in a calm state. Wolfing lunch or breakfast down as quickly as possible while answering emails or staring at a screen causes harm to the digestive process.

Instead, appreciate your meal and connect with what you're doing. It'll make all the difference.

Hydrate, Hydrate, Hydrate
Dehydration is a leading cause of fatigue.
We don't drink enough. We just don't.

We also take on toxins that dehydrate us further - that extra cup of coffee to keep you going because you're tired, or that glass of wine at the end of the day. This puts added stress on our adrenals and kidneys that increase our overall stress and toxic load.

Our bodies get confused and disorientated in a dehydrated state, and instead of recognising thirst, we get signals that we're tired or hungry. Next time you feel like this, have a glass of water before reaching for a snack and see how you feel.

A great 'drink more water' hack is to buy a litre bottle of water, fill it and have it at your desk. Aim to drink at least one before lunch and one after lunch.

Curb the Coffee

Try not to go crazy on the coffee.

You may be attached to the coffee filter by a drip to get through the day, but it's not solving any of your fatigue issues. If anything, it may be contributing to them.

If you are one of those people that claim caffeine has no effect on you, just be aware it has an impact on your gut health. It can cause both stomach acidity issues and intestinal permeability, which will lead to further health disturbances.

Caffeine also stresses the adrenal glands by encouraging them to produce more of the hormone cortisol. Chronic overuse can lead to an over-production of this hormone that will leave you feeling really out of whack and exhausted.

I'm not suggesting you don't touch the stuff ever again, but do be aware just how much you're drinking; 2 cups, maybe 3, should be your limit.

The time of day you reached for that last cup of Joe will make all the difference. Caffeine has a half-life of approximately 5 hours. So if you consumed 40 milligrams of caffeine at 4pm, you would still have 20mg remaining in your system at 9pm. This will impact on the quality of your sleep.

If you're finding falling and staying asleep difficult, try to limit caffeine to the morning - no coffee or tea (including green tea) after midday or 2pm at the latest.

Just One Glass of Wine

A glass of wine has actually been shown to be beneficial at reducing stress levels within the body. This is amplified if it's combined with a social activity, like meeting a friend or sharing a meal. However, this benefit does not apply to the whole bottle.

Alcohol disrupts sleep. Period. Even if you think it knocks you out and you get to sleep easily after a few drinks, it is not helping you get that high quality sleep that you need to heal and wake refreshed.

Drinking too much regularly can lead to gut dysbiosis. This is where the bad guys outweigh the good guys in your gut, leaving you open to a whole lot of health problems. If you are drinking more than 2 glasses of alcohol a day, you are putting yourself at risk with your gut health.

It's easy to get caught up into having a couple beers or glasses of wine every evening, but be aware of what a measure is and set some limits and disciplines for yourself. Whatever your drinking habits are, see how you can cut back. You need to look at what you're drinking now, be honest with yourself, and then make a commitment.

When it comes to other drugs including weed, speed, sleeping pills, cigarettes, or whatever, just remember they often give short term relief but make things harder over the long term.

If you have questions or want added accountability around this, or anything else, you can head over to the free community for leaders here: tiny.cc/leadersgroup.

Sleep

When the results of my survey started coming in, I was surprised by how many people are having issues sleeping.

Underlying stress is a major culprit in sleep disruption.

Chronic, long-term stress has a damaging effect on the body leading to a gradual decline in health over time.. Rapid change or a sudden influx of stress wreaks havoc physically and mentally too. Stress = overthinking and rumination = can't turn your brain off to sleep = more stress because you can't sleep. It's a vicious cycle that's hard to break.

CASE STUDY

One individual shared how, in the past, he had always fallen immediately asleep each night. However, since lockdown began, he has had issues sleeping, especially on Sunday evening - right before the work week starts.

He admitted that while he isn't feeling stressed about any particular thing, the world events have been worrying him. This is a classic case of low-level background stress.

Here are a few of my hacks to help encourage a deeper, more refreshing sleep;

» **Journalling.** Empty your mind by taking a black notebook and writing out anything that is bothering you. Don't worry if it's legible, you don't have to read it back. This practise is meant to get things out; out of your mind and out of your consciousness so you can let it go. If it's nothing you need to keep, tear up the pages and burn them, throw them away or flush them down the toilet. It's cathartic to literally flush your thoughts away.

» **Charge your phone in a different room.** Put it on silent and get it away from your bed. Whatever you do, don't keep it underneath your pillow. Cut the cord between you and your emails/messages/social media, they can wait until you're up and running in the morning. EMF's (electromagnetic frequencies) and the blue light put unnecessary stress on the body and disrupt your natural circadian rhythms.

» **Routine.** Go to sleep and wake up at the same time every day. Try to schedule at least a 7 and a half hour sleep. Set the alarm and DON'T use snooze. After two weeks your body should automatically get up at that time.

» **Deep breathing technique.** When you first wake up, place your hands on the abdomen and inhale into the hands so your belly rises. Exhale and repeat 5 times. Then get up, go to the bathroom and splash cold water on your face. This tones the vagus nerve and can help balance the nervous system.

» **Bedtime snack.** If you have trouble with your blood sugar, having a small snack before you go to bed could make all the difference. Try half a banana, or an apple with a tablespoon of nut butter, or a few unsalted, raw nuts. Something small and balanced in fat, protein and carbs can help stabilise your levels throughout the night and allow you to wake refreshed and raring to go in the morning.

» **No distractions.** Make sure you aren't watching TV, working, playing games, or reading in bed. You should train your body that bed is for sleeping only...well, for sleeping and maybe one other thing...

Mindfulness

Mindfulness and meditation are ways to maintain a positive and constructive outlook.

Incorporating a short meditation practice can transform your day in the short term, and your life in the long-term.

A common misconception is thinking that if your mind has been busy during the meditation, it means that you were doing it wrong.

Meditation is a skill that needs to be cultivated over time, just like exercise. If you've never run before, you don't go out and run a marathon on your first jog. You're also not going to become that enlightened being with a quiet mind on your first attempt at meditating. (If you do, get in contact - I'd love some tips.)

I've had a daily meditation practise for more than 10 years (typically 20 to 30 minutes a day), and my mind still chirps at me most of the way through it.

I can also tell you that meditation has brought peace, calmness, and positivity to my life. It seems to slow things down around me. I see everything much more clearly. This enables me to make a measured response instead of a flash reaction.

From a leadership standpoint, meditation has been a game-changer. I can keep my cool and make better decisions.

There are so many different styles of meditation, and a variety of apps offering thousands of guided meditations - calm, insight timer and brain tap are a few. You can also look for a meditation teacher if you prefer to work directly with someone.

Exercise

Exercise can substantially affect your physical, mental and emotional health.

I'm not saying you need to be an olympic athlete to be happy and healthy. There are many uncomplicated, free and easy ways to incorporate sneaky exercise into your day.

Here are a few of my exercise hacks to a healthier life:

» **Yoga/stretch.** First thing in the morning I take 10 minutes to do some light stretching or yoga. Here's a free YouTube video that I often use: https://www.youtube.com/watch?v=dRsC1YdXqOc It's short and sweet, and I feel great afterwards. There are many accounts on youtube with short, accessible stretchy yoga videos if you don't like that one - keep looking.

» **Daily Walk.** in the afternoon, after eating lunch, I like to go on a 30-minute walk. I'd recommend leaving your phone at home and walk alone with your thoughts. This is a meditation, especially if it's a walk in nature. A few days a week you could listen to an audio book, a podcast or some music. It needs to be something to break up your day and allow you to detach from the morning. Getting outside and away from the screen is essential to integrate into the day, especially in the winter months when we don't get much sunshine.

Routines

Having a regular routine morning and night can keep you at your best.

Here are the basics of a morning routine you can take and tailor for your specific situation;

» **Wake up.** Take a few minutes to ease into the day. Stay phone free for the first 30 minutes - no emails, no messages, no scrolling. Get up and out of bed.

» **Breathe.** Go to an undisturbed, quiet area in your house. Spend 2 - 5 minutes listening to your breath, focusing on the sensation of inhaling and exhaling. This is a meditation technique that will bring you into the present moment.

» **Move your body.** Spend 10 minutes stretching, either intuitively or follow a short morning yoga video.

» **Get ready.** Shower, get dressed and ready for your day. Even if you're working at home - you are long past the "work in your jam jams" stage. By looking sharp and actively dressing in professional attire, you are signalling to your body and your mind that you are ready to work.

» **Breakfast.** Always try to eat undistracted. Focus on the food and family/social interaction if you live with other people. Enjoying and appreciating your surroundings sends positive signals to your nervous system, which is then able to relax and calm down.

After breakfast, you can check your phone. I promise you won't have missed anything, it'll all still be there waiting and ready for you.

I strongly recommend scheduling a 45 minute lunch every day. When you do go for lunch - be it 5 minutes or 45, leave your workstation. Physically get away from the area you have been working. It's crucial to mentally detach too, perhaps flick through a magazine or newspaper, plug into a fun podcast or that new album you've been meaning to listen to.

Go for a walk around your neighborhood. The world won't end if you've taken an actual lunch break. Getting outside and moving your body will revitalize your energy levels and stimulate your mind.

Return to work refreshed, focused and ready to power through the rest of the afternoon - rather than dragging yourself through another day with your eyes fixated on the clock.

Fun

The hardest thing about lockdown for me was nothing to look forward to. It brought me down that there wasn't anything in the calendar that excited me.

After a discussion with my wife, we decided that every 90 days we would book an Airbnb somewhere in the UK to get out of town for the weekend. Having these little trips booked gave me something to look forward to, opposed to the calendar stretching out into endless bland uncertainty.

These trips are the "big things" to look forward to every few months. Equally as important are the "little things" that bring you enjoyment on a daily or weekly basis.

Is there a hobby you used to love but lost the time for? Is there something that you've always wanted to have a go at, but life got in the way? Perhaps it's learning to paint, or picking up a musical instrument, or maybe building model aeroplanes or finally setting up that train set that's been in the attic for years. Even a great fiction book does it for me.

It's about getting involved in something that isn't work-related in your time off; something that you can look forward to developing and engaging with. Applying yourself and rediscovering that joy can be a sanity check and a mental health boost.

Positivity

I was on the train to London, and I got caught up in reading all the pre-election news from the US. By the time my hour-long trip into Waterloo was over, my mood was low.

I even called my wife to discuss the whole sorry situation. She stopped me mid grumble and asked what I had been looking at on the train ride. It all clicked into place, and I was able to reflect upon the cause of my sudden blues. It really brought home the fact that what we read and consume has a direct impact on our mood.

Every day we are exposed to a million different triggers that can bring about either a positive or negative reaction.

Be conscious of what you are exposed to and the effect this can have on the mind and body. Scrolling through endless negative media content without a break can really trash your state of mind, leaving you drained and fatigued.

We have power over the mind. Perception is everything; look for the worst in something, and I can guarantee you will find it. Equally, look for the best in something, and I can guarantee you will find it. You can literally shift the patterns of your brain from the negative to the positive with brain conditioning techniques.

Starting a daily gratitude list is one way to encourage this shift in mindset. All you need to do is write down 3 things every day that you are grateful for. They don't need to be profound or life-altering, and you don't have to spend hours mulling it over. It can be something like, "I had a really great catch up with Barb on my team today". Of course, you can make them more profound if you like, but appreciating the small achievements in the day can be enough to power your overall positivity too.

The more specific you can be the better. For example, I might begin with "I'm grateful for my wife", but then really honing in on the specifics of my gratitude that day, I would say, "I'm grateful for that kiss my wife gave me right before dinner." Neurologically, this creates a connection to the event that fires up and opens pathways in the brain - this is positive reinforcement.

Over time, you'll catch yourself naturally gravitating towards this positive mindset, and even keeping a mental checklist throughout the day of all the moments you've enjoyed. You are training your brain to focus on the positive things in life. It's easier and far more common to dwell on the negative.

Your brain will increase with what you focus on, and there's so much positive content out there that can uplift you. If you want positive news, check out authors like Stephen Pinker or Peter Diamandis. These are people that are focused on solutions and not problems.

You can curate the content you're exposed to. Make sure you're letting some light in there too.

Control

Being out of control of a situation can generate stress, and we often find ourselves in times or scenarios that we have no control over.

We do, however, have control of ourselves, our behaviours, and responses. We always have a choice on what impulse to act on.

The next time you're feeling stressed or overwhelmed, write down what is in your control and what is out of your control. Break it down and work out the root cause. Think about where your energy is going.

The Core 10

These are the 10 tools to set yourself up every single day. These tools will enable you to manage your energy fuel tank, and bring your best to the table as far as positivity, energy, confidence, and resilience are concerned.

The first five are before the working day starts and the last 5 can occur anytime at your leisure.

1. 10 Minutes of Stretching
2. 5 Minutes of silence
3. Shower
4. Dress Professionally
5. Healthy Breakfast

    Pre-phone

    ****

    Post phone

6. Healthy Lunch
7. Walked Outside for at least 10 minutes
8. Help Someone Else
9. Do Something Enjoyable
10. Appreciate ONE Thing about your life

Printed in Great Britain
by Amazon